Reservoir Dogs

QUENTIN TARANTINO

D1393245

faber and faber

First published in 1996
by Faber and Faber Limited
3 Queen Square London WC1N 3AU

This edition published in 2000

Photoset by Parker Typesetting Service, Leicester
Printed and bound in Great Britain by
Mackays of Chatham PLC, Chatham, Kent

A CIP record for this book
is available from the British Library

ISBN 0-571-20279-9

10 9 8 7 6 5 4 3 2 1

R

Contents

Quentin Tarantino: Answers First, Questions Later
An interview with Graham Fuller,   ix

RESERVOIR DOGS,   1

Credits,   110

RESERVOIR DOGS was first shown at the 1992 Cannes Film Festival. The cast includes:

MR WHITE (Larry)	Harvey Keitel
MR ORANGE (Freddy)	Tim Roth
MR BLONDE (Vic)	Michael Madsen
NICE GUY EDDIE	Chris Penn
MR PINK	Steve Buscemi
JOE CABOT	Lawrence Tierney
HOLDAWAY	Randy Brooks
MARVIN NASH	Kirk Baltz
MR BLUE	Eddie Bunker
MR BROWN	Quentin Tarantino
TEDDY	Michael Sottile
SHOT COP	Robert Ruth
YOUNG COP	Lawrence Bender

Casting by	Ronnie Yeskel
Music Supervisor	Karyn Rachtman
Costume Designer	Betsy Heimann
Production Designer	David Wasco
Editor	Sally Menks
Director of Photography	Andrzej Sekula
Executive Producers	Richard N. Gladstein
	Ronna B. Wallace
	Monte Hellman
Co-Producer	Harvey Keitel
Producer	Lawrence Bender
Written and Directed by	Quentin Tarantino

Quentin Tarantino (photo by Paul Joyce)

Quentin Tarantino: Answers First, Questions Later

Quentin Tarantino was born in Knoxville, Tennessee, in 1963, the year when Monte Hellman's *Back Door to Hell* and *Flight to Fury*, Don Siegel's *The Killers*, and Sergio Leone's *A Fistful of Dollars* were also in gestation – as Tarantino himself could probably tell you. The writer/director of *Reservoir Dogs* (1992) and *Pulp Fiction* (1990), as well as the writer of *True Romance* (1993) and *Natural Born Killers* (1994), Tarantino is the most extreme instance of a movie-struck kid who has parlayed his obsession with cheap thrillers and Westerns into a career at a time when both forms are being reinvented and revitalized by Hollywood.

Tarantino was raised by his mother in Southern California and received his movie education at the Carson Twin Cinema, Scottsdale, and later as an employee of Video Archives, Manhattan Beach, where he worked while training as an actor. His scripts pullulate with references to his movie diet during those days. The story of two kids, Clarence (Christian Slater) and Alabama (Patricia Arquette), on the run with a cache of cocaine they've offloaded from the Mob, *True Romance*, directed by Tony Scott, is set up by Tarantino as a self-conscious analogue to Terrence Malick's *Badlands*, replete with the same Erik Satie theme and a gauche voice-over by the female lead.

The point is that Tarantino is not so much a post-modern *auteur* as a *post*-post-modern one, for he is feverishly interested in pop-cultural artefacts and ideas (television, rock music, comics, and junk food, as well as movies) that themselves spring from earlier incarnations or have already been mediated or predigested. Because *Badlands* was made with *They Drive By Night*, *You Only Live Once*, *Gun Crazy*, and James Dean in mind, *True Romance* has a double frame of reference. In *Reservoir Dogs* – Tarantino's update on Stanley Kubrick's *The Killing* and/or Larry Cohen's *Q* – the pre-heist debate about the possible meanings of Madonna's 'Like a Virgin', as implausible as it is funny, is an anti-intellectual demystification of Madonna's much chewed-over status as a post-feminist icon in books like *Madonnarama: Essays on Sex and Popular Culture*. It's not Madonna that concerns Tarantino in this scene – but what Madona has come to represent.

All of which might seem like mere dressage for Tarantino's tough, cynical, and exuberantly amoral genre-bending scripts. Except that his appreciation of pop ephemera is as central to his movies – you could say it is the world they move in – as their rabidly talky flow, their intricately structured plots, their casual explosions of violence, and their reverse psychology. (Brought together in anonymity, for example, *Reservoir Dogs*' hoods form immediate allegiances, while the coolest among them turns out to be a psychopathic killer and the angriest the most professional.) That delight in contradiction is really Tarantino's calling card, for he writes pulp movies for audiences who want more than mere visceral thrills, who may not have read much Tolstoy, and even less Michael Crichton or John Grisham, but who might figure out how bloody a 'Douglas Sirk steak' can be, or the qualitative difference between *Bewitched* and *I Dream of Jeannie* – to cite Tarantino's *Pulp Fiction*. This was the script he had just finished writing, for himself to direct, when we talked, in May 1993.

GRAHAM FULLER: *When you started writing scripts, was it as a means to becoming a director or because you had specific stories you wanted to tell as a screenwriter?*

QUENTIN TARANTINO: I've never considered myself a writer writing stuff to sell, but as a director who writes stuff for himself to direct. The first script I ever did was *True Romance*. I wrote it to do it the way the Coen Brothers did *Blood Simple*, and I almost directed it. Me and a friend, Roger Avary, were going to raise about $1.2 million, form a limited partnership and then go off and make the movie. We worked on it for three years, trying to get it off the ground like that, and it never worked. I then wrote *Natural Born Killers*, again hoping to direct it myself, this time for half-a-million dollars – I was shooting lower and lower. After a year and a half I was no further along than at the beginning. It was then out of frustration that I wrote *Reservoir Dogs*. I was going to go really guerrilla style with it, like the way Nick Gomez did *Laws of Gravity*. I'd lost faith in anyone giving me money – and then that's *when* I got the money.

GF: *What was your response to relinquishing* True Romance *and* Natural Born Killers *as scripts you would direct yourself?*

QT: After *Reservoir Dogs* I was offered both of them to direct. The producers who had *Natural Born Killers* – before Oliver Stone acquired it – tried like hell to talk me into directing it. Tony Scott and Bill Unger had *True Romance*. I had convinced Tony to direct it, but Bill was saying, 'Look, Quentin, would you be interested in doing this as a follow-up to *Reservoir Dogs*?' And my answer was no. I didn't want to do either one of them because they were both written to be my first film and by then I'd made my first film. I didn't want to go backwards and do old stuff. I think of them as like old girlfriends: I loved them but I didn't want to marry them any more. The thing that I am the happiest about is that the first film of mine produced was one that I directed.

GF: *How had you originally gone about positioning yourself in the industry?*

QT: During the time I wrote these things, I wasn't anywhere near the industry. Eventually, what got me inside was moving to Hollywood and making some friends who were film-makers. One of them was Scott Speigel, who had just written the Clint Eastwood movie, *The Rookie* [1990], and people were calling him to write things he didn't have time to do, so he would suggest me. The next thing I knew, I was sending out *True Romance* and *Natural Born Killers* as audition scripts and, little by little, I started doing a little rewrite at this company, doing a little dialogue polishing at that one.

GF: *You say you're not a writer, but the narratives of each of your scripts is very carefully crafted and rich in imagery. You establish your characters very fast.*

QT: I'm not trying to be falsely modest. I am a pretty good writer – but I always think of myself as a director.

GF: *In the* Natural Born Killers *script you wrote in a lot of the camera directions, so it was clearly a blueprint for a film you'd direct yourself. I remember Ken Russell saying he gets irritated when he sees scripts telling him where to put the camera.*

QT: Writing for somebody else and writing a movie for yourself to do are completely different. I'm not bagging on screenwriters, but if I was a full-on writer, I'd write novels.

GF: *You've talked about directors that have influenced you – including Samuel Fuller, Douglas Sirk, and Jean-Pierre Melville – but were you also influenced by specific screenwriters or novelists?*

QT: I think Robert Towne is one screenwriter who deserves every little bit of the reputation he has. I'm also a fan of Charles B. Griffith, who used to write for Roger Corman. But most of my writing heroes are novelists. When I wrote *True Romance*, I was really into Elmore Leonard. In fact, I was trying to write an Elmore Leonard novel as a movie, though I'm not saying it's as good.

GF: *What about earlier writers? Is your script for* Pulp Fiction *modelled on Cain, Chandler, and Hammett?*

QT: I don't know how much I am actually influenced by those guys, but I have read them all and I like them. The idea behind *Pulp Fiction* was to do a *Black Mask* movie – like that old detective story magazine. But I just finished the script and it's really not like that at all; it kind of went somewhere else. Two othe⁻ writers I'm crazy about are Ben Hecht and Charles MacArthur, both as playwrights and as screenwriters. In fact, on the first page of *Pulp Fiction*, I describe two characters talking in 'rapid-fire motion, like in *His Girl Friday*'.

GF: *How do your screenplays evolve?*

QT: One of the main things I like to do with my scripts is monkey with structure a little bit. I always know the structure I am going to employ in advance, and all the whys and the wherefores of the story when I start writing, but there's always some unanswered questions, ideas I want to explore. I don't know how effective they're going to be, but I want to try them out. When I start writing I let the characters take over. If you read my scripts, you'll see that the dialogue scenes just go on and on and on. I never went to a screenwriting or creative writing class, but I did study acting for about six years and I actually approach writing the way an actor approaches acting.

GF: *Do you write in a linear way?*

QT: I have to write from beginning to end because the characters are kind of telling the story.

GF: True Romance's *narrative is linear, but with your script for* Natural Born Killers, *you wove in a lot of flashbacks and a long sequence involving a tabloid-TV-film-in-progress. Then you made another leap forward with* Reservoir Dogs, *which has a kind of dovetailed structure.*

QT: *True Romance* had a more complicated structure to start with, but when the producers bought the script they cut-and-pasted it into a linear form. The original structure was also an answers-first, questions-later structure, like *Reservoir Dogs*. Thinking back on it, that version probably wasn't the most effective script that I've done, but I still think it would have worked. Tony [Scott] actually started putting it together that way in the editing room, but he said it didn't work for him.

I guess what I'm always trying to do is use the structures that I see in novels and apply them to cinema. A novelist thinks nothing of starting in the middle of a story. I thought that if you could figure out a cinematic way to do that, it would be very exciting. Generally, when they translate novels to movies, that's the first stuff that goes out. I don't do this to be a wise guy or to show how clever I am. If a story would be more dramatically engaging if you told it from the beginning, or the end, then I'd tell it that way. But the *glory* is in pulling it off my way.

GF: *When you sat down to write* Reservoir Dogs, *did you have a structure or a stratagem in your head?*

QT: Definitely. I wanted the whole movie to be about an event we don't see, and I wanted it all to take place at the rendezvous at the warehouse – what would normally be given ten minutes in a heist film. I wanted the whole movie to be set there and to play with a real-time clock as opposed to a movie clock ticking. I also wanted to introduce these guys in a series of chapters. Like, when you're reading a book, you're reading about Moe, Larry and Curly doing something in chapters one, two, and three, and then chapter four is about Moe five years before. Then, when that chapter is over, you're back in the main thrust of the action again, but now you know a little bit more about this guy than you did before.

GF: *Did* Reservoir Dogs *go through rewrites?*

QT: Not really. I wrote it real quick, and six months after I wrote it, we were shooting it. After I did the first draft, the big change I made was to include the scene where Mr Orange is in the bathroom telling his story – that whole undercover-cop training sequence. I had written it earlier and then, when I was putting the script together, I thought, 'No one cares about this; they want to get back to the warehouse.' So I left it out and put it in my drawer. But when we were trying to get the movie made, I dug it out and read it and I went, 'Quentin, are you insane? This is really good. You've got to put this in.' That was the only major change to the second draft.

I also kept changing who said what in the opening scene. That was the thing that went through the most metamorphosis. At one time, Mr

Blonde made this speech, and another time Mr White said it, and so-and-so said this and so-and-so said that. I just kept switching speeches all the time. It's really funny, because when I look at it now, it doesn't look like it went through all that. But maybe it was good that it did – because all the right people ended up saying all the right things.

GF: *Did you have to fix things during shooting at all?*

QT: The only thing I did was a little polish after auditions, because auditioning shows you what lines don't work. So I got rid of them. Also, actors will come in and either improvise deliberately or they'll accidentally say something and it's funny.

GF: *I don't know if you've ever seen Michael Powell and Emeric Pressburger's* The Life and Death of Colonel Blimp . . .

QT: I never have – I've always wanted to.

GF: *The key event in the first half of the film is a duel between Roger Livesey and Anton Walbrook. There's a great deal of rigmarole leading up to it concerning the rules and codes of duelling. Then, just at the moment the duel is about to start, the camera cranes away from it and you never actually see it. It functions in the film in the same way the heist functions in* Reservoir Dogs. *My question is: do you consider omission part of the art of screenwriting? Is what you leave out as crucial as what you put in?*

QT: I completely think so. To me, it even applies to the way you frame a shot. What you don't see in the frame is as important as what you do see. Some people like to show everything. They don't want the audience to have a second guess about anything; it's *all* there. I'm not like that. I've seen so many movies that I like playing around with them. Pretty much nine out of ten movies you see let you know in the first ten minutes what kind of movie it's going to be, and I think the audience subconsciously reads this early ten-minute message and starts leaning to the left when the movie is getting ready to make a left turn; they're predicting what the movie is going to do. And what I like to do is use that information against them.

GF: *Do you feel that your screenplays provide a kind of legitimate forum for violence?*

QT: I don't quite look at it like that. I don't take the violence very seriously. I find violence very funny, and especially in the stories that I've been telling recently. Violence is part of this world and I am drawn to the outrageousness of real-life violence. It isn't about people lowering people from helicopters on to speeding trains, or about terrorists hijacking something or other. Real-life violence is, you're in a restaurant and a man and his wife are having an argument and all of a sudden the guy gets so mad at her, he picks up a fork and stabs her in the face. That's really crazy and comic-bookish – but it also *happens*; that's how real violence comes kicking and screaming into your perspective in real life. I am interested in the act, in the explosion, and in the entire aftermath of that. What do we do after this? Do we beat up the guy who stabbed the woman? Do we separate them? Do we call the cops? Do we ask for our money back because our meal has been ruined? I am interested in answering all those questions.

GF: *What about the visual aesthetics of violence, which seem to be writ large in your films? In John Woo's films, for instance, the violence is pleasurable to watch if you accept it as stylized comic-strip violence.*

QT: Well, like I say, I get a kick out of violence in movies. The worst thing about movies is, no matter how far you can go, when it comes to violence you are wearing a pair of handcuffs that novelists, say, don't wear. A writer like Carl Hiassen can do whatever he wants. The more outrageous, the better for his books. In movies, you don't really have that freedom.

GF: *When I asked you if your films provide a legitimate forum for violence, what I meant was that – within reason, obviously – it can be acceptable to see on screen that which is unpalatable in real life.*

QT: Oh, I completely agree with that. To me, violence is a totally aesthetic subject. Saying you don't like violence in movies is like saying you don't like dance sequences in movies. I do like dance sequences in movies, but if I didn't, it doesn't mean I should stop dance sequences from being made. When you're doing violence in movies, there's going to be a lot of people who aren't going to like it, because it's a mountain they can't climb. And they're not *jerks*. They're just not into that. And they don't *have* to be into it. There's other things that they can see. If you *can* climb that mountain, then I'm going to give you something to climb.

GF: *Conventional notions of morality are made complicated in your films. You give your characters a license to kill.*

QT: I'm not trying to preach any kind of morals or get any kind of message across, but for all the wildness that happens in my movies, I think that they usually lead to a moral conclusion. For example, I find what passes between Mr White and Mr Orange at the end of

Reservoir Dogs very moving and profound in its morality and its human interaction.

GF: *Why do you think pop culture, comics, and movies themselves proliferate in your scripts?*

QT: I guess it just comes from me, from what I find fascinating. If I have an interesting take on it, it's not that I'm necessarily lacing it with irony or showing it to you so you can laugh at it. I'm trying to show the enjoyment of it.

GF: *Junk food, too.*

QT: Cap'n Crunch cereal or whatever! It's funny, because I'm actually getting on a more nutritious diet myself. I started writing down this list of bad fast-food restaurants I'd go to to eat a bunch of stuff that I really didn't want to eat. I'm looking at it right now in my apartment and it says, 'Stay away until you absolutely have to go there. Then enjoy it. But don't get used to it.' Then there's a list that says, 'Hanging out with Scott, Roger, and this group of guys!'

GF: *Scott and Roger being the prototypes for the TV crew guys with those names in* Natural Born Killers?

QT: Yeah. And then underneath it says, 'I want to still do that, but I must not do it frequently, and cut down in other areas, so I can still have fun with those guys.' And then another bad place: 'The kitchen at the office' – Cokes and cookies and stuff like that; stay away from there. Empty calories.

GF: *Do you see yourself writing scripts in a more classical style, perhaps less charged with pop-cultural references, and perhaps less frenetic. A period film?*

QT: I don't necessarily want to make anything less frenetic. Not right now. I'll give you an example. L. M. Kit Carson let me read his script for *The Moviegoer*, and indicated that it would be cool by him if I wanted to direct it. I read it and I liked it a lot, but I told him, 'I'm not mature enough to make this movie right now.' Not that the work I'm doing is immature, but I'm still on my own road. Eventually, I'll get off it and want to go in a different direction, or do somebody else's work.

GF: *What has changed about your writing since you began?*

QT: I think it's more sophisticated. I am not chasing it as much. I know the effects I'm after, and I eventually get them. I trust myself more that it will all work out – just keep the characters talking to each other and they'll find the way. After you've done it a few times, you fly blind for a little while, not knowing how you're going to wrap a script up, and then at the last minute something really cool happens. Constantly, what happens in my scripts is that the characters will do something that just blows me away. With regard to the torture scene in *Reservoir Dogs*, I try to explain to people that I didn't sit down and say, 'OK, I'm gonna write this really bitchin' torture scene.' When Mr Blonde reached into his boot and pulled out a straight razor, I didn't know he had a straight razor in his boot. I was surprised. That happens all the time when I'm writing. I equate it to acting. If you're improvising, all of a sudden you say or do something that puts this charge into a scene. That's what it's like writing. The other thing I've learned through acting is that whatever's affecting you that day needs to find a way to be filtered into the work that you're doing. Because if it doesn't, you're denying it.

Basically, I don't come up with any new ideas. I have a stockpile of ideas in my head that goes back five or six years, and when it comes time to write another script or to think about what I want to do next as a writer, I flip through them and find the right one. They're incubating. I'll come up with one of them and say, 'OK, it's not this one's time yet. Let it just sit here and get a little better. Let's do this one instead.' I want to do them all eventually; I know I never will.

GF: *Do your stories come fully formed?*

QT: I always start with scenes I know I am going to put in and scenes from scripts I never finish. Every script I have written has at least twenty pages that are taken from other things I've done. I had the idea for *Pulp Fiction* a long time ago and then I came up with the idea of how to do it in the editing room when we were cutting *Reservoir Dogs*. I thought about it and thought about it, way past the point I normally do. Normally when I can't think about anything else but the script, then I write it. I couldn't do it while I was in the lab but I finally moved to Amsterdam for a couple of months and started writing *Pulp Fiction* there. After thinking about it for six or seven months straight, suddenly what I was writing was completely different. Even though the movie takes place in Los Angeles, I was taking in all this weird being-in-Europe-for-the-first-time stuff and that was finding its way into the script. So some genre story that I'd had for five years started becoming very personal as I wrote it. That's the only way I know how to make the work any good – make it personal.

GF: *How many drafts will you do before you hand it in?*

QT: When I hand in the first draft of a script, it's probably my third draft of it. That's why I'm pretty comfortable with it and can say, 'If you don't like it, then you don't want to do it, because this is what I'm going to do.'

GF: *Do you revise as you proceed, or do you go back and redo the whole thing?*

QT: I revise scenes as I go along, minimally. Usually, I'm just trying to keep going on it.

GF: *Do you write overnight?*

QT: I write into the night.

GF: *On a word processor?*

QT: No, I don't know how to type properly. When I know I'm going to do a script, I'll go to the stationery store and buy a notebook with eighty or a hundred pages in it, where you rip the pages out of the ring file, and I'll say, 'OK, this is the notebook I'm going to write *Pulp Fiction* or whatever in.' I also buy three red felt pens and three black felt pens. I make this big ritual out of it. It's just psychology. I always say that you can't write poetry on a computer, but I can take this notebook places, I can write in restaurants, I can write in friends' houses, I can write standing up, I can write lying down in my bed – I can write everywhere. It never looks like a script; it always looks like Richard Ramirez's diary, the diary of a madman. When I get to my last stage, which is the typing stage, it starts looking like a script for the first time. Then I start making dialogue cuts and fixing up things that didn't work before.

GF: *Do you enjoy the process?*

QT: I usually think it's going to be horrible, but I always have a great time.

GF: *Does it pour out?*

QT: If it doesn't, then I just don't do it that day. If I can't get the characters talking, then I ain't gonna do it. If it's *me* making the characters talk to each other, then that's phoney baloney. It becomes exciting when a character says something and I'm like, 'Wow, he said this? I didn't know that he had a wife or I didn't know he felt like that!'

GF: *So it's a process of discovering what's locked away inside there?*

QT: Very much so. That's why I could *never* do a script treatment where you take the story from beginning to end. I'm not that kind of a writer. There's questions I don't want to answer until I get to writing.

(Abridged from a longer interview that appeared in *Projections 3*)

RESERVOIR DOGS

INT. UNCLE BOB'S PANCAKE HOUSE — MORNING

Eight men dressed in BLACK SUITS, sit around a table at a breakfast café. They are Mr White, Mr Pink, Mr Blue, Mr Blonde, Mr Orange, Mr Brown, Nice Guy Eddie Cabot, and the big boss, Joe Cabot. Most are finished eating and are enjoying coffee and conversation. Joe flips through a small address book. Mr Brown is telling a long and involved story about Madonna.

MR BROWN

'Like a Virgin' is all about a girl who digs a guy with a big dick. The whole song is a metaphor for big dicks.

MR BLONDE

No, it's not. It's about a girl who is very vulnerable and she's been fucked over a few times. Then she meets some guy who's really sensitive –

MR BROWN

– Whoa . . . whoa . . . time out, Greenbay. Tell that bullshit to the tourists.

JOE
(looking through his address book)
Toby . . . who the fuck is Toby? Toby . . . Toby . . . think . . . think . . . think . . .

MR BROWN

It's not about a nice girl who meets a sensitive boy. Now granted that's what 'True Blue' is about, no argument about that.

MR ORANGE

Which one is 'True Blue?'

NICE GUY EDDIE

You don't remember 'True Blue'? That was a big ass hit for Madonna. Shit, I don't even follow this Tops in Pops shit, and I've at least heard of 'True Blue'.

MR ORANGE

Look, asshole, I didn't say I ain't heard of it. All I asked was how does it go? Excuse me for not being the world's biggest Madonna fan.

3

MR WHITE

I hate Madonna.

MR BLUE

I like her early stuff. You know, 'Lucky Star', 'Borderline' – but once she got into her 'Papa Don't Preach' phase, I don't know, I tuned out.

MR BROWN

Hey, fuck all that, I'm making a point here. You're gonna make me lose my train of thought.

JOE

Oh fuck, Toby's that little china girl.

MR WHITE

What's that?

JOE

I found this old address book in a jacket I ain't worn in a coon's age. Toby what? What the fuck was her last name?

MR BROWN

Where was I?

MR PINK

You said 'True Blue' was about a nice girl who finds a sensitive fella. But 'Like a Virgin' was a metaphor for big dicks.

MR BROWN

Let me tell ya what 'Like a Virgin''s about. It's about some cooze who's a regular fuck machine. I mean all the time, morning, day, night, afternoon, dick, dick, dick, dick, dick, dick, dick, dick, dick, dick, dick.

MR BLUE

How many dicks was that?

MR PINK

A lot.

MR BROWN

Then one day she meet a John Holmes motherfucker, and it's like, whoa baby. This mother fucker's like Charles Bronson in 'The Great Escape'. He's diggin' tunnels. Now she's gettin' this serious dick action, she's feelin' something she ain't felt since forever. Pain.

JOE

Chew? Toby Chew? No.

MR BROWN

It hurts. It hurts her. It shouldn't hurt. Her pussy should be Bubble-Yum by now. But when this cat fucks her, it hurts. It hurts like the first time. The pain is reminding a fuck machine what it was like to be a virgin. Hence, 'Like a Virgin'.

The fellas crack up.

JOE

Wong?

MR BROWN

Fuck you, wrong. I'm right! What the fuck do you know about it anyway? You're still listening to Jerry-fucking-Vale records.

JOE

Not wrong, dumb ass, Wong! You know, like the Chinese name?

Mr White snatches the address book from Joe's hand. They fight, but they're not really mad at each other.

MR WHITE

Give me this fuckin' thing.

JOE

What the fuck do you think you're doin'? Give me my book back!

MR WHITE

I'm sick of fuckin' hearin' it; Joe, I'll give it back when we leave.

JOE

Whaddaya mean, give it to me when we leave, give it back now.

MR WHITE

For the past fifteen minutes now, you've just been droning on with names. 'Toby . . . Toby . . . Toby . . . Toby Wong . . . Toby Wong . . . Toby Chung . . . fuckin' Charlie Chan.' I got Madonna's big dick outta my right ear, and Toby Jap I-don't-know-what, outta my left.

JOE

What do you care?

MR WHITE

When you're as annoying as hell, I care a lot.

JOE

Give me my book.

MR WHITE

You gonna put it away?

JOE

I'm gonna do whatever I wanna do with it.

MR WHITE

Well, then, I'm afraid I'm gonna have to keep it.

MR BLONDE

Joe, you want me to shoot him for you?

MR WHITE

Shit, you shoot me in a dream, you better wake up and apologize.

NICE GUY EDDIE

Have you guys been listening to K-Billy's super sounds of the seventies weekend?

MR PINK

Yeah, it's fuckin' great, isn't it?

NICE GUY EDDIE

Can you believe the songs they been playin'?

MR PINK

You know what I heard the other day? 'Heartbeat – It's Lovebeat' by little Tony DeFranco and the DeFranco Family. I haven't heard that since I was in fifth fuckin' grade.

NICE GUY EDDIE

When I was coming down here, I was playin' it. And 'The Night the Lights Went Out in Georgia' came on. Now I ain't heard that song since it was big, but when it was big I heard it a million-trillion times. I'm listening to it this morning, and this was the first time I ever realized that the lady singing the song, was the one who killed Andy.

MR BROWN

You didn't know Vicki Lawrence killed the guy?

NICE GUY EDDIE

I thought the cheatin' wife shot Andy.

MR BLONDE

They say it in the song.

NICE GUY EDDIE

I know, I heard it. I musta zoned out whenever that part came on before. I thought when she said that little sister stuff, she was talkin' about her sister-in-law, the cheatin' wife.

JOE

No, she did it. She killed the cheatin' wife, too.

MR WHITE

Who gives a damn?

The table laughs. The Waitress comes over to the table. She has the check, and a pot of coffee.

WAITRESS

Can I get anybody more coffee?

JOE

No, we're gonna be hittin' it. I'll take care of the check.

She hands the bill to him.

WAITRESS

Here ya go. Please pay at the register, if you wouldn't mind.

JOE

Sure thing.

WAITRESS

You guys have a wonderful day.

They all mutter equivalents. She exits and Joe stands up.

JOE

I'll take care of this, you guys leave the tip.

(*to Mr White*)
And when I come back, I want my book back.

MR WHITE

Sorry, it's my book now.

JOE

Blue, shoot this piece of shit, will ya?

Mr Blue shoots Mr White with his finger. Mr White acts shot. Joe exits.

NICE GUY EDDIE

Okay, everybody cough up green for the little lady.

Everybody whips out a buck, and throws it on the table. Everybody, that is, except Mr Pink.

C'mon, throw in a buck.

MR PINK

Uh-uh. I don't tip.

NICE GUY EDDIE

Whaddaya mean, you don't tip?

MR PINK

I don't believe in it.

NICE GUY EDDIE

You don't believe in tipping?

MR BROWN
(*laughing*)
I love this guy, he's a madman, this guy.

MR BLONDE

Do you have any idea what these ladies make? They make shit.

MR PINK

Don't give me that. She don't make enough money, she can quit.

Everybody laughs.

NICE GUY EDDIE

I don't even know a Jew who'd have the balls to say that. So let's get this straight. You never ever tip?

MR PINK

I don't tip because society says I gotta. I tip when somebody
deserves a tip. When somebody really puts forth an effort, they
deserve a little something extra. But this tipping automatically,
that shit's for the birds. As far as I'm concerned, they're just doin'
their job.

MR BLUE

Our girl was nice.

MR PINK

Our girl was okay. She didn't do anything special.

MR BLUE

What's something special, take ya in the kitchen and suck your
dick?

They all laugh.

NICE GUY EDDIE

I'd go over twelve percent for that.

MR PINK

Look, I ordered coffee. Now we've been here a long fuckin' time,
and she's only filled my cup three times. When I order coffee, I
want it filled six times.

MR BLONDE

What if it's too busy?

MR PINK

The words 'too busy' shouldn't be in a waitress's vocabulary.

NICE GUY EDDIE

Excuse me, Mr Pink, but the last thing you need is another cup of
coffee.

They all laugh.

MR PINK

These ladies aren't starvin' to death. They make minimum wage.
When I worked for minimum wage, I wasn't lucky enough to have
a job that society deemed tipworthy.

NICE GUY EDDIE

Ahh, now we're getting down to it. It's not just that he's a cheap bastard –

MR ORANGE

– It is that too –

NICE GUY EDDIE

– It is that too. But it's also he couldn't get a waiter job. You talk like a pissed-off dishwasher: 'Fuck those cunts and their fucking tips.'

MR BLONDE

So you don't care that they're counting on your tip to live?

Mr Pink rubs two of his fingers together.

MR PINK

Do you know what this is? It's the world's smallest violin, playing just for the waitresses.

MR WHITE

You don't have any idea what you're talking about. These people bust their ass. This is a hard job.

MR PINK

So's working at McDonalds, but you don't feel the need to tip them. They're servin' ya food, you should tip 'em. But no, society says tip these guys over here, but not those guys over there. That's bullshit.

MR BLUE

They work harder than the kids at McDonalds.

MR PINK

Oh yeah, I don't see them cleaning fryers.

MR BLUE

These ladies are taxed on the tips they make. When you stiff 'em, you cost them money.

MR WHITE

Waitressing is the number one occupation for female non-college graduates in this country. It's the one job basically any woman can get, and make a living on. The reason is because of tips.

MR PINK

Fuck all that.

They all laugh.

MR PINK

Hey, I'm very sorry that the government taxes their tips. That's fucked up. But that ain't my fault. It would appear that waitresses are just one of the many groups the government fucks in the ass on a regular basis. You show me a paper says the government shouldn't do that, I'll sign it. Put it to a vote, I'll vote for it. But what I won't do is play ball. And this non-college bullshit you're telling me, I got two words for that: 'Learn to fuckin' type.' 'Cause if you're expecting me to help out with the rent, you're in for a big fuckin' surprise.

MR ORANGE

He's convinced me. Give me my dollar back.

Everybody laughs. Joe comes back to the table.

JOE

Okay ramblers, let's get to rambling. Wait a minute, who didn't throw in?

MR ORANGE

Mr Pink.

JOE
(to Mr Orange)

Mr Pink?

(to Mr Pink)

Why?

MR ORANGE

He don't tip.

JOE
(to Mr Orange)

He don't tip?

(to Mr Pink)

You don't tip? Why?

11

MR ORANGE

He don't believe in it.

JOE
(to Mr Orange)

He don't believe in it?

(to Mr Pink)

You don't believe in it?

MR ORANGE

Nope.

JOE
(to Mr Orange)

Shut up!

(to Mr Pink)

Cough up the buck, ya cheap bastard, I paid for your goddam breakfast.

MR PINK

Because you paid for the breakfast, I'm gonna tip. Normally I wouldn't.

JOE

Whatever. Just throw in your dollar, and let's move.
(to Mr White)

See what I'm dealing with here. Infants. I'm fuckin' dealin' with infants.

The eight men get up to leave. Mr White's waist is in the foreground. As he buttons his coat, for a second we see he's carrying a gun. They exit Uncle Bob's Pancake House, talking amongst themselves.

*[TITLE CARD:

'ONE OF THESE MEN IS A COP.'

Then underneath it:

'AND BY THE END, ALL BUT ONE WILL BE DEAD.']

* Cut from completed film.

EXT. UNCLE BOB'S PANCAKE HOUSE – DAY

CREDIT SEQUENCE:

When the credit sequence is finished, fade to black.

Over the black we hear the sound of someone screaming in agony.

Under the screaming, we hear the sound of a car hauling ass, through traffic.

Over the screams and the traffic noise, we hear somebody else say:

> SOMEBODY ELSE
> (*off*)
>
> Just hold on buddy boy.

Somebody stops screaming long enough to say:

> SOMEBODY
> (*off*)
>
> I'm sorry. I can't believe she killed me. Who would've fuckin' thought that?

CUT TO:

INT. GETAWAY CAR (MOVING) – DAY

The Somebody screaming is Mr Orange. He lies in the backseat. He's been shot in the stomach. Blood covers both him and the backseat.

Mr White is the Somebody Else. He's behind the wheel of the getaway car. He's easily doing 80 mph, dodging in and out of traffic. Though he's driving for his life, he keeps talking to his wounded passenger in the backseat.

They are the only two in the car.

> MR WHITE
>
> Hey, just cancel that shit right now! You're hurt. You're hurt really fucking bad, but you ain't dying.

> MR ORANGE
> (*crying*)
>
> All this blood is scaring the shit outta me. I'm gonna die, I know it.

14

MR WHITE

Oh excuse me, I didn't realize you had a degree in medicine. Are you a doctor? Are you a doctor? Answer me please, are you a doctor?

MR ORANGE

No, I'm not!

MR WHITE

Ahhhh, so you admit you don't know what you're talking about. So if you're through giving me your amateur opinion, lie back and listen to the news. I'm taking you back to the rendezvous, Joe's gonna get you a doctor, the doctor's gonna fix you up, and you're gonna be okay. Now say it: you're gonna be okay. *Say it*: you're gonna be okay!

Mr Orange doesn't respond. Mr White starts pounding on the steering wheel.

MR WHITE

Say-the-goddam-words: you're gonna be okay!

MR ORANGE

I'm okay.

MR WHITE
(*softly*)

Correct.

INT. WAREHOUSE – DAY

The Camera does a 360 around an empty warehouse. Then the door swings open, and Mr White carries the bloody body of Mr Orange inside.

Mr Orange still is moaning loudly from his bullet hit.

Mr White lays him down upon a mattress on the floor.

MR WHITE

Just hold on, buddy boy. Hold on, and wait for Joe. I can't do anything for you, but when Joe gets here, which should be any time now, he'll be able to help you. We're just gonna sit here, and wait for Joe. Who are we waiting for?

MR ORANGE

Joe.

MR WHITE

Bet your sweet ass we are.

MR ORANGE

Larry, I'm so scared, would you please hold me.

Mr White very gently embraces the bloody Mr Orange. Cradling the young man, Mr White whispers to him.

MR WHITE
(*whispering*)

Go ahead and be scared, you've been brave enough for one day. I want you to just relax now. You're not gonna die, you're gonna be fine. When Joe gets here, he'll make ya a hundred percent again.

Mr White lays Mr Orange back down. He's still holding his hand. Mr Orange looks up at his friend.

MR ORANGE

Look, I don't wanna be a fly in the ointment, but if help doesn't come soon, I gotta see a doctor. I don't give a fuck about jail, I just don't wanna die.

MR WHITE

You're not gonna fucking die, all right?

MR ORANGE

I wasn't born yesterday. I'm hurt, and I'm hurt bad.

MR WHITE

It's not good . . .

MR ORANGE

Hey, bless your heart for what you're trying to do. I was panicking for a moment, but I've got my senses back now. The situation is, I'm shot in the belly. And without medical attention, I'm gonna die.

MR WHITE

I can't take you to a hospital.

MR ORANGE

Fuck jail! I don't give a shit about jail. But I can't die. You don't have to take me in. Just drive me up to the front, drop me on the sidewalk. I'll take care of myself. I won't tell them anything. I swear to fucking God, I won't tell 'em anything. Look in my eyes, look right in my eyes.

(*Mr White does*)

I-won't-tell-them-anything. You'll be safe.

MR WHITE

Lie back down, and try to –

MR ORANGE

I'm going to die! I need a doctor! I'm begging you, take me to a doctor.

MR WHITE

Listen to me, kid. You ain't gonna die! Along with the kneecap, the gut is the most painful area a guy can get shot in.

MR ORANGE

No shit.

MR WHITE

But it takes a long time to die from it. I'm talkin' days. You'll wish you were dead, but it takes days to die from your wound. Time is on your side. When Joe gets here, he'll have a doctor patch you up in nothin' flat. You know how Joe operates. He's got MD's in his back pocket. Just bite the fuckin' bullet and wait for Joe to get here.

Mr Orange lays his head back. He quietly mutters to himself:

MR ORANGE

Take me to a doctor, take me to a doctor, please.

Suddenly, the warehouse door bursts open and Mr Pink steps inside.

MR PINK

Was that a fucking set-up or what?

Mr Pink sees Mr Orange on the floor, shot and bloody.

MR PINK

Oh fuck, Orange got tagged.

Throughout this scene, we hear Mr Orange moaning.

MR WHITE

Gut shot.

MR PINK

Oh that's just fucking great! Where's Brown?

MR WHITE

Dead.

MR PINK

Goddam, goddam! How did he die?

MR WHITE

How the fuck do you think? The cops shot him.

MR PINK

Oh this is bad, this is so bad.
                      (referring to Mr Orange)
Is it bad?

MR WHITE

As opposed to good?

MR PINK

This is so fucked up. Somebody fucked us big time.

MR WHITE

You really think we were set up?

MR PINK

You even doubt it? I don't think we got set up, I know we got set up!
I mean really, seriously, where did all those cops come from, huh?
One minute they're not there, the next minute they're there. I
didn't hear any sirens. The alarm went off, okay. Okay, when an
alarm goes off, you got an average of four minutes response time.
Unless a patrol car is cruising that street, at that particular moment,
you got four minutes before they can realistically respond. In one
minute there were seventeen blue boys out there. All loaded for
bear, all knowing exactly what the fuck they were doing, and they
were all just there! Remember that second wave that showed up in
the cars? Those were the ones responding to the alarm, but those
other motherfuckers were already there, they were waiting for us.
                        (pause)
You haven't thought about this?

MR WHITE

I haven't had a chance to think. First I was just trying to get the fuck
outta there. And after we got away, I've just been dealin' with him.

MR PINK

Well, you better start thinking about it. 'Cause I, sure as fuck, am
thinking about it. In fact, that's all I'm thinking about. I came this
close to just driving off. Whoever set us up, knows about this place.
There could've been cops sitting here waiting for me. For all we
know, there's cops, driving fast, on their way here now.

MR WHITE

Let's go in the other room.

*The camera creeps along a wall, coming to a corner. We move past it, and
see down a hall.*

At the end of the hall is a bathroom. The bathroom door is partially closed, restricting our view. Mr Pink is obscured, but Mr White is in view.

MR PINK
(*off*)

What the fuck am I doing here? I felt funny about this job right off. As soon as I felt it I should have said 'No thank you', and walked. But I never fucking listen. Every time I ever got burned buying weed, I always knew the guy wasn't right. I just felt it. But I wanted to believe him. If he's not lyin' to me, and it really is Thai stick, then whoa baby. But it's never Thai stick. And I always said if I felt that way about a job, I'd walk. And I did, and I didn't, because of fuckin' money!

MR WHITE

What's done is done, I need you cool. Are you cool?

MR PINK

I'm cool.

MR WHITE

Splash some water on your face. Take a breather.

We hear the sink running, and Mr Pink splashing water on his face. He takes out his gun and lays it on the counter.

I'm gonna get me my smokes.

Mr White opens the bathroom door, walks down the hall, and out of frame. We see Mr Pink, his back turned towards us, bent over the sink. Then he grabs a towel, and dries his face. Mr White enters frame with a pack of Chesterfields in his hand.

Want a smoke?

MR PINK

Why not?

The two men light up.

MR WHITE

Okay, let's go through what happened. We're in the place, everything's going fine. Then the alarm gets tripped. I turn around

and all these cops are outside. You're right, it was like, bam! I blink my eyes and they're there. Everybody starts going apeshit. Then Mr Blonde starts shootin' all the –

MR PINK

– That's not correct.

MR WHITE

What's wrong with it?

MR PINK

The cops didn't show up after the alarm went off. They didn't show till after Mr Blonde started shooting everyone.

MR WHITE

As soon as I heard the alarm, I saw the cops.

MR PINK

I'm telling ya, it wasn't that soon. They didn't let their presence be known until after Mr Blonde went off. I'm not sayin' they weren't there, I'm sayin' they were there. But they didn't move in till Mr Blonde became a madman. That's how I know we were set up. You can see that, can't you, Mr White?

MR WHITE

Look, enough of this 'Mr White' shit –

MR PINK

– Don't tell me your name, I don't want to know! I sure as hell ain't gonna tell ya mine.

MR WHITE

You're right, this is bad.

(*pause*)

How did you get out?

MR PINK

Shot my way out. Everybody was shooting, so I just blasted my way outta there.

CUT TO:

EXT. CROWDED CITY STREET – DAY

Mr Pink is hauling ass down a busy city sidewalk. He has a canvas bag with a shoulder strap in one hand, and a .357 Magnum in the other. If any bystanders get in his way, he just knocks them down. We dolly at the same speed, right alongside of him.

Four Policemen are running after Mr Pink. Three are running together, and one fat one is lagging a few paces behind. We dolly with them.

In his mad dash Mr Pink runs into the street, and is hit by a moving car.

He's thrown up on the hood, cracking the windshield, and rolling off.

INT. CAR (STOPPED) – DAY

The camera is in the backseat. A shocked woman is the car's driver. Mr Pink pulls himself up from the hood, shakes himself off, and points his magnum at the driver.

MR PINK

Get outta the car! Get the fuck outta the car!

The Shocked Woman starts screaming.

Mr Pink tries to open the driver's side door, but it's locked.

MR PINK

Open the fucking door!

EXTREME CU – DRIVER'S SIDE WINDOW

Mr Pink SMASHES it in our face.

EXT. STREET – DAY

Dolly with Cops coming up fast.

Mr Pink drags the Shocked Woman out of the car.

The Cops reach the corner, guns aimed.

Using the car as a shield, Mr Pink fires three shots at the Cops.

Everybody hits the ground, or scatters.

Cops fire. Mr Pink unloads his gun.

Fat Cop is shot in his pot belly, falls back in the arms of a Young Cop. The Fat Cop screams in pain, the Young Cop screams in anguish.

Mr Pink hops in the car. Cops fire.

INT. CAR (MOVING) – DAY

Camera in the backseat, Mr Pink floors it. Speeding down the street, with the Cops firing after him.

EXT. STREET – DAY

The Young Cop takes off running and firing after the getaway car. It's no use. Mr Pink leaves him in the dust.

BACK TO:

INT. BATHROOM – DAY

Mr Pink and Mr White still talking in the bathroom.

MR PINK

Tagged a couple of cops. Did you kill anybody?

MR WHITE

A few cops.

MR PINK

No real people?

MR WHITE

Uh-uh, just cops.

MR PINK

Could you believe Mr Blonde?

MR WHITE

That was one of the most insane fucking things I've ever seen.
Why the fuck would Joe hire somebody like that?

MR PINK

I don't wanna kill anybody. But if I gotta get out that door, and
you're standing in my way, one way or the other, you're gettin'
outta my way.

MR WHITE

That's the way I look at it. A choice between doin' ten years, and
takin' out some stupid motherfucker, ain't no choice at all. But I
ain't no madman either. What the fuck was Joe thinkin'? You
can't work with a guy like that. We're awful goddamn lucky he
didn't tag us, when he shot up the place. I came this fucking
close –
    (holds up two fingers and makes a tiny space between them)
– to taking his ass out myself.

MR PINK

Everybody panics. When things get tense, everybody panics.
Everybody. I don't care what your name is, you can't help it. It's
human nature. But ya panic on the inside. Ya panic in your head.
Ya give yourself a couple a seconds of panic, then you get a grip
and deal with the situation. What you don't do, is shoot up the
place and kill everybody.

MR WHITE

What you're supposed to do is act like a fuckin' professional. A
psychopath is not a professional. You can't work with a
psychopath, 'cause ya don't know what those sick assholes are

gonna do next. I mean, Jesus Christ, how old do you think that black girl was? Twenty, maybe twenty-one?

MR PINK

Did ya see what happened to anybody else?

MR WHITE

Me and Mr Orange jumped in the car and Mr Brown floored it. After that, I don't know what went down.

MR PINK

At that point it became every man for himself. As far as Mr Blonde or Mr Blue are concerned, I ain't got the foggiest. Once I got out, I never looked back.

MR WHITE

What do you think?

MR PINK

What do I think? I think the cops caught them, or killed 'em.

MR WHITE

Not even a chance they punched through? You found a hole.

MR PINK

Yeah, and that was a fucking miracle. But if they did get away, where the fuck are they?

MR WHITE

You don't think it's possible, one of them got a hold of the diamonds and pulled a –

MR PINK

Nope.

MR WHITE

How can you be so sure?

MR PINK

I got the diamonds.

MR WHITE

Where?

MR PINK

I stashed 'em. You wanna go with me and get 'em? Sure, we can go right now, we can leave this second. I think we should have our fuckin' heads examined for waiting around here.

MR WHITE

That was the plan, we meet here.

MR PINK

Then where is everybody? I say the plan became null and void once we found out we got a rat in the house. We ain't got the slightest fuckin' idea what happened to Mr Blonde or Mr Blue. They could both be dead or arrested. They could be sweatin' 'em, down at the station house right now. Yeah they don't know our names, but they can sing about this place.

MR WHITE

I swear to god I'm fuckin' jinxed.

MR PINK

What?

MR WHITE

Two jobs back, it was a four-man job, we discovered one of the team was an undercover cop.

MR PINK

No shit?

MR WHITE

Thank God, we discovered in time. We hadda forget the whole fuckin' thing. Just walked away from it.

MR PINK

So who's the rat this time? Mr Blue? Mr Blonde? Joe? It's Joe's show, he set this whole thing up. Maybe he set it up to set it up.

MR WHITE

I don't buy it. Me and Joe go back a long time. I can tell ya straight up, Joe definitely didn't have anything to do with this bullshit.

MR PINK

Oh, you and Joe go back a long time. I known Joe since I was a kid. But me saying Joe definitely couldn't have done it is ridiculous. I can say I definitely didn't do it, 'cause I know what I

27

did or didn't do. But I can't definitely say that about anybody else, 'cause I don't definitely know. For all I know, you're the rat.

MR WHITE

For all I know, you're the rat.

MR PINK

Now you're using your head. For all we know, he's the rat.

MR WHITE

That kid in there is dying from a fuckin' bullet that I saw him take. So don't be calling him a rat.

MR PINK

Look, asshole, I'm right! Somebody's a fuckin' rat. How many times do I hafta say it before it sinks in your skull.

The talking stops. The two men just stare at each other. Mr Pink breaks the silence.

MR PINK

I gotta take a squint, where's the commode in this dungeon?

MR WHITE

Go down the hall, turn left, up those stairs, then turn right.

Mr Pink exits frame, leaving Mr White alone.

CUT TO:

TITLE CARD:

'MR WHITE'

EMPTY FRAME

In the background we see what looks like an office set up.

VOICE

How's Alabama?

MR WHITE

Alabama? I haven't seen Bama over a year and a half.

VOICE

I thought you two were a team.

We were for a little while. Did about four jobs together. Then decided to call it quits. You push it long enough that woman man thing gets in your way after a while.

We now cut to see Joe behind his desk.

JOE

What's she doin' now?

MR WHITE

She hooked up with Fred McGar, they've done a coupla jobs together. Helluva woman. Good little thief. *[I heard tell you tied the knot with a gorgeous gal.

JOE
(*laughs*)

Tammy's a looker all right.

MR WHITE

I heard she's from Arkansas.

JOE

Tennessee. Knoxville, Tennessee. She used to be a regular on *Hee-Haw*. You know that country show with all those fuckin' hicks.

MR WHITE

I know what *Hee-Haw* is.
(*pause*)
So why did ya marry her?

JOE

I love her. Pretty silly, an old fart like me, huh?

MR WHITE

It's kinda silly. It's kinda cute, too.

JOE

You know what's really silly? She loves me back. I know you won't believe that, but I don't give a damn, because I know she does. You know what she's got me doin', Larry, readin' books. She'll read somethin', come to me and say, 'Joe' – in that funny accent she has, sounds like Li'l Abner – 'Joe, I just read this book

* Cut from completed film.

and it's really good. And I want you to read it, 'cause I want to talk with you about it.' And if I know what's good for me, I better read it. I'm turnin' into a regular bookworm. I always got a paperback with me.

Joe opens his desk and throws a dogeared paperback of The Bell Jar *on the desk. Mr White looks at it.*

JOE

Ya ever read it?

Mr White shakes his head.

Tammy loves that Sylvia Plath. I ain't so sure, myself. She killed herself, ya know.

MR WHITE

Tammy?

JOE

No, asshole, Plath. The woman who wrote the goddamn book. Look, I know everybody thinks I'm a chump, but they're wrong and I'm right. I know how she feels about me, and how she makes me feel when I'm with her. And that's good enough for me.

MR WHITE

Plath?

Joe gives White a hard look. Mr White laughs.

What's hard to believe? You're a lovable guy. In fact, Joe, I'd go so far as to describe you as a catch.

JOE
(laughing)
Keep needling me, Weisenheimer, and you're gonna meet Mr Boot.

Mr White walks over to the side of the desk.

MR WHITE

We've met. And Mr Butt wants to stay far away.] So, explain the telegram.

JOE

Five-man job. Bustin' in and bustin' out of a diamond wholesaler's.

MR WHITE

Can you move the ice afterwards? I don't know nobody who can move ice.

Not a problem, got guys waitin' for it. But what happened to
Marcellus Spivey? Didn't he always move your ice?

MR WHITE

He's doin' twenty years in Susanville.

JOE

What for?

MR WHITE

Bad luck. What's the exposure like?

JOE

Two minutes, tops. It's a tough two minutes. It's daylight, during
business hours, dealing with a crowd. But you'll have the guys to
deal with the crowd.

MR WHITE

How many employees?

JOE

Around twenty. Security pretty lax. They almost always just deal
in boxes. Rough uncut stones they get from the syndicate. On a
certain day this wholesaler's gettin' a big shipment of polished
stones from Israel. They're like a way station. They're gonna get
picked up the next day and sent to Vermont.

MR WHITE

No they're not.

The men share a laugh.

What's the cut, poppa?

JOE

Juicy, junior, real juicy.

FADE TO BLACK

BACK TO THE GARAGE

*We follow Mr Pink, handheld, back through the rooms and hallways to
the garage. We follow behind him up to Mr White, who's standing over
Mr Orange.*

MR PINK

So, I don't know about you, but me – I'm gonna split, check into a motel and lay low for a few days.

As he gets closer he sees Mr Orange is out. He runs over to them.

Holy shit, did he fuckin' die on us?

Mr White doesn't respond.

So, is he dead or what?

MR WHITE

He ain't dead.

MR PINK

So what is it?

MR WHITE

I think he's just passed out.

MR PINK

He scared the fuckin' shit outta me. I thought he was dead fer sure.

Mr White stands up and walks over to a table.

MR WHITE

He will be dead fer sure, if we don't get him to a hospital.

MR PINK

We can't take him to a hospital.

MR WHITE

Without medical attention, this man won't live through the night. That bullet in his belly is my fault. Now while that might not mean jack shit to you, it means a helluva lot to me. And I'm not gonna just sit around and watch him die.

MR PINK

Well, first things first, staying here's goofy. We gotta book up.

MR WHITE

So what do you suggest, we go to a hotel? We got a guy who's shot in the belly, he can't walk, he bleeds like a stuck pig, and when he's awake, he screams in pain.

MR PINK

You gotta idea, spit it out.

MR WHITE

Joe could help him. If we can get in touch with Joe, Joe could get him to a doctor, Joe could get a doctor to come and see him.

During Mr Pink's dialogue, we slowly zoom in to a closeup of Mr White.

MR PINK
(*off*)

Assuming we can trust Joe, how we gonna get in touch with him? He's supposed to be here, but he ain't, which is making me nervous about being here. Even if Joe is on the up and up, he's probably not gonna be that happy with us. Joe planned a robbery, but he's got a blood bath on his hands now. Dead cops, dead robbers, dead civilians . . . Jesus Christ! I tend to doubt he's gonna have a lot of sympathy for our plight. If I was him, I'd try and put as much distance between me and this mess as humanly possible.

MR WHITE

Before you got here, Mr Orange was askin' me to take him to a hospital. Now I don't like turning him over to the cops, but if we don't, he's dead. He begged me to do it. I told him to hold off till Joe got here.

MR PINK
(*off*)

Well Joe ain't gettin' here. We're on our own. Now, I don't know a goddamn body who can help him, so if you know somebody, call 'em.'

MR WHITE

I don't know anybody.

MR PINK
(*off*)

Well, I guess we drop him off at the hospital. Since he don't know nothin' about us, I say it's his decision.

MR WHITE'S POV:

CLOSEUP – MR PINK

> MR WHITE
> (*off*)
>
> Well, he knows a little about me.

> MR PINK
>
> You didn't tell him your name, did ya?

> MR WHITE
> (*off*)
>
> I told him my first name, and where I'm from.

There is a long silence and a blank look from Mr Pink, then he screams:

> MR PINK
>
> Why?

> MR WHITE
> (*off*)
>
> I told him where I was from a few days ago. It was just a casual conversation.

> MR PINK
>
> And what was telling' him your name when you weren't supposed to?

> MR WHITE
> (*off*)
>
> He asked.

Mr Pink looks at Mr White as if he's retarded.

We had just gotten away from the cops. He just got shot. It was my fuckin' fault he got shot. He's a fuckin' bloody mess – he's screaming. I swear to God, I thought he was gonna die right then and there. I'm tryin' to comfort him, telling him not to worry, he's gonna be okay, I'm gonna take care of him. And he asked me what my name was. I mean, the man was dyin' in my arms. What the fuck was I supposed to tell him, 'Sorry, I can't give out that information, it's against the rules. I don't trust you enough?' Maybe I shoulda, but I couldn't.

MR PINK

Oh, I don't doubt it was quite beautiful –

MR WHITE
(off)

Don't fuckin' patronize me.

MR PINK

One question: Do they have a sheet on you, where you told him
you're from?

MR WHITE
(off)

Of course.

MR PINK

Well that's that, then. I mean, I was worried about mug shot
possibilities already. But now he knows: (a) what you look like (b)
what your first name is, (c) where you're from and (d) what your
speciality is. They ain't gonna hafta show him a helluva lot of
pictures for him to pick you out. That's it, right? You didn't tell
him anything else that could narrow down the selection?

MR WHITE
(off)

If I have to tell you again to back off, me an' you are gonna go round
and round.

*Mr Pink walks out of the closeup and turns his back on Mr White. Mr
White's POV pans over to him.*

MR PINK

We ain't taking him to a hospital.

MR WHITE
(off)

If we don't, he'll die.

MR PINK

And I'm very sad about that. But some fellas are lucky, and some ain't.

MR WHITE
(off)

That fuckin' did it!

38

Mr White's POV charges toward Mr Pink.

Mr Pink turns toward him in time to get punched hard in the mouth.

END OF POV

Mr White and Mr Pink have a very ungraceful and realistic fight. They go at each other like a couple of alley cats.

As Mr White swings and punches, he screams:

MR WHITE

You little motherfucker!

Mr Pink yells as he hits:

MR PINK

Ya wanna fuck with me?! You wanna fuck with me?! I'll show you who you're fuckin' with!

The two men end up on the floor kicking and scratching. Mr White gets Mr Pink in a headlock.

Mr Pink reaches in his jacket for his gun, and pulls it out. Mr White sees this, immediately lets go of Mr Pink, and goes for his own weapon.

The two men are on the floor, on their knees, with their guns outstretched, aiming at one another.

MR WHITE
You wanna shoot me, you little piece of shit? Take a shot!

MR PINK

Fuck you, White! I didn't create this situation, I'm just dealin'
with it. You're actin' like a first-year fuckin' thief. I'm actin' like a
professional. They get him, they can get you, they get you, they
get closer to me, and that can't happen. And you, you
motherfucker, are lookin' at me like it's my fault. I didn't tell him
my name. I didn't tell him where I was from. I didn't tell him
what I knew better than to tell him. Fuck, fifteen minutes ago,
you almost told me your name. You, buddy, are stuck in a
situation you created. So, if you wanna throw bad looks
somewhere, throw 'em at a mirror.

Mr Pink lowers his gun.

Then from off screen we hear:

VOICE

You kids don't play so rough. Somebody's gonna start crying.

INT. WAREHOUSE – DAY – MEDIUM CLOSEUP ON MR BLONDE

The Voice belongs to the infamous Mr Blonde.

Mr Blonde leans against a pole, drinking a fast-food Coke.

MR PINK

Mr Blonde! You okay? We thought you might've gotten caught.
What happened?

Mr Blonde doesn't answer.

He stares at Mr Pink and Mr White, sipping his Coke.

*This is making Pink and White nervous as hell. But Mr Pink tries to talk
through it.*

Really, how did you get away?

Silence from Mr Blonde.

Where's Mr Blue?

Silence.

We were hopin' you two would be together.

Silence.

We were worried the cops got ya.

Silence.

Look, Brown is dead, Orange got it in the belly.

MR WHITE

Enough! You better start talkin' to us, asshole, 'cause we got shit
we need to talk about. We're already freaked out, we need you
actin' freaky like we need a fuckin' bag on our hip.

Mr Blonde looks at his two partners in crime, then moves towards them.

MR BLONDE

So, talk.

MR WHITE

We think we got a rat in the house.

MR PINK

I guarantee we got a rat in the house.

MR BLONDE

What would ever make you think that?

MR WHITE

Is that supposed to be funny?

MR PINK

We don't think this place is safe.

MR WHITE

This place just ain't secure any more. We're leaving, and you
should go with us.

MR BLONDE

Nobody's going anywhere.

*Silence takes over the room. Mr Blonde stops moving. After a few beats
the silence is broken.*

MR WHITE
(*to Mr Pink*)

Piss on this turd, we're outta here.

Mr White turns to leave.

MR BLONDE

Don't take another step, Mr White.

Mr White explodes, raising his gun and charging towards Mr Blonde.

MR WHITE

Fuck you, maniac! It's your fuckin' fault we're in so much trouble.

Mr Blonde calmly sits down. He looks to Mr Pink.

MR BLONDE
(*referring to Mr White*)

What's this guy's problem?

MR WHITE

What's my problem? Yeah, I gotta problem. I gotta big problem with any trigger-happy madman who almost gets me shot!

MR BLONDE

What're you talkin' about?

MR WHITE

That fuckin' shooting spree in the store.

MR BLONDE

Fuck 'em, they set off the alarm, they deserve what they got.

MR WHITE

You almost killed me, asshole! If I had any idea what type of guy you were, I never would've agreed to work with you.

MR BLONDE

You gonna bark all day, little doggie, or are you gonna bite?

MR WHITE

What was that? I'm sorry, I didn't catch it. Would you repeat it?

MR BLONDE
(*calm and slow*)

I said: 'Are you gonna bark all day, doggie, or are you gonna bite.'

MR PINK

Both of you two assholes knock it the fuck off and calm down!

MR WHITE
(*to Mr Blonde*)

So you wanna git bit, huh?

MR PINK

Cut the bullshit, we ain't on a fuckin' playground!
(*pause*)
I don't believe this shit, both of you got ten years on me, and I'm
the only one actin' like a professional. You guys act like a bunch
of fuckin' niggers. You ever work a job with a bunch of niggers?
They're just like you two, always fightin', always sayin' they're
gonna kill one another.

MR WHITE
(*to Mr Pink*)

You said yourself, you thought about takin' him out.

MR PINK

Then. That time has passed. Right now, Mr Blonde is the only
one I completely trust. He's too fuckin' homicidal to be workin'
with the cops.

MR WHITE

You takin' his side?

MR PINK

Fuck sides! What we need is a little solidarity here. Somebody's
stickin' a red hot poker up our asses and we gotta find out whose
hand's on the handle. Now I know I'm no piece of shit . . .
(*referring to Mr White*)

And I'm pretty sure you're a good boy . . .
(*referring to Mr Blonde*)
And I'm fuckin' positive you're on the level. So let's figure out
who's the bad guy.

Mr White calms down and puts his gun away.

MR BLONDE

Well, that was sure exciting.
(*to Mr White*)
You're a big Lee Marvin fan, aren't you? Me too. I don't know
about the rest of you fellas, but my heart's beatin' fast.

44

>   (*pause for a beat*)
> Okay, you guys, follow me.

Mr Blonde hops out of his chair and heads for the door.

The other two men just follow him with their eyes.

                        MR WHITE

Follow you where?

                        MR BLONDE

Down to my car.

                        MR WHITE

Why?

                        MR BLONDE

It's a surprise.

Mr Blonde walks out the door.

EXT. WAREHOUSE – DAY

Three cars are parked out front. Mr Blonde is walking towards the car he drove. Mr White and Mr Pink are walking behind. The camera is handheld following behind them.

                        MR PINK
We still gotta get out of here.
                        MR BLONDE
We're gonna sit here and wait.

                        MR WHITE

For what, the cops?
                        MR BLONDE
Nice Guy Eddie.
                        MR PINK
Nice Guy Eddie? What makes you think Nice Guy's anywhere but on a plane half way to Costa Rica?
                        MR BLONDE
'Cause I just talked to him. He's on his way down here, and nobody's going anywhere till he gets here.

You talked to Nice Guy Eddie? Why the fuck didn't you say that in the first place?

MR BLONDE

You didn't ask.

MR WHITE

Hardy-fuckin'-har. What did he say?

MR BLONDE

Stay put. Okay, fellas, take a look at the little surprise I brought you.

Mr Blonde opens up the trunk of his car. A handcuffed, uniformed policeman is curled up inside the trunk.

MR BLONDE

Since we gotta wait for Nice Guy anyway, let's talk to our boy in blue here and see if he knows anything about this rat business.

The three crooks share a frightening laugh. We slowly zoom into a close up of the cop.

CUT TO:

TITLE CARD:

'MR BLONDE'

INT. JOE CABOT'S OFFICE – DAY

We're inside the office of Joe Cabot. Joe's on the phone, sitting behind his desk.

JOE
(*into phone*)

Sid, I'm tellin' you don't worry about it. You had a bad couple of months, it happens.

(*pause*)

Sid . . . Stop, you're embarrassing me. I don't need to be told what I already know. When you have bad months, you do what every businessman in the world does, I don't care if he's J. P. Morgan or Irving the tailor. Ya ride it out.

There's a knock on Cabot's office door.

Come in.

One of Cabot's goons, Teddy, opens the door and steps inside. Cabot covers the receiver with his hand and looks towards the man.

> TEDDY

Vic Vega's outside.

> JOE

Tell him to come in.

Teddy leaves.

> *(into phone)*

Sid, a friend of mine's here. I gotta go.

> *(pause)*

Good enough, bye.

He hangs up the phone, stands, and walks around to the front of his desk.

Teddy opens the office door, and Toothpick Vic Vega walks in.

Toothpick Vic Vega is none other than our very own Mr Blonde. Vic is dressed in a long black leather seventies style jacket.

Joe stands in front of his desk with his arms open.

The two men embrace. Teddy leaves, closing the door behind him.

> JOE

How's freedom, kid, pretty fuckin' good, ain't it?

> VIC

It's a change.

> JOE

Ain't that a sad truth. Remy Martin?

> VIC

Sure.

> JOE

Take a seat.

Joe goes over to his liquor cabinet. Vic sits in a chair set in front of Joe's desk.

47

(while he pours the drinks)
Who's your parole officer?

                          VIC

A guy named Scagnetti. Seymour Scagnetti.

                          JOE

How is he?

                          VIC

Fuckin' asshole, won't let me leave the halfway house.

Joe finishes pouring the drink; walks over and hands it to Vic.

                          JOE

Never ceases to amaze me. Fuckin' jungle bunny goes out there, slits some old woman's throat for twenty-five cents. Fuckin' nigger gets Doris Day as a parole officer. But a good fella like you gets stuck with a ball-bustin' prick.

Joe walks back around his desk and sits in his chair. Vic swallows some Remy.

                          VIC

I just want you to know, Joe, how much I appreciated your care packages on the inside.

                          JOE

What the hell did you expect me to do? Just forget about you?

                          VIC

I just wanted you to know, they meant a lot.

                          JOE

It's the least I could do, Vic. I wish I coulda done more.
                    (Joe flashes a wide grin at Vic)
Vic. Toothpick Vic. Tell me a story. What're your plans?

                          VIC

Well, what I wanna do is go back to work. But I got this Scagnetti prick deep up my ass. He won't let me leave the halfway house till I get some piece of shit job. My plans have always been to be part of the team again.

There's a knock at the door.

                          JOE

Come in.

The door opens and in walks Joe's son, Nice Guy Eddie. Vic turns around in his seat and sees him.

EDDIE
(*to Vic*)
I see ya sittin' here, but I don't believe it.

Vic gets out of his seat and hugs Eddie.

How ya doin', Toothpick?

VIC
Fine, now.

EDDIE
I'm sorry man, I shoulda picked you up personally at the pen. This whole week's just been crazy. I've had my head up my ass the entire time.

VIC
Funny you should mention it. That's what your father and I been talkin' about.

EDDIE
That I should've picked you up?

No. That your head's been up your ass. I walk through the door
and Joe says, 'Vic, you're back, thank god. Finally somebody
who knows what the fuck he's doing. Vic, Vic, Vic, Eddie, my
son, is a fuck up.' And I say, 'Well, Joe, I coulda told you that.'
'I'm ruined! My son, I love him, but he's taking my business and
flushing it down the fuckin' toilet!'

(to Joe)

I'm not tellin' tales out of school. You tell 'im Joe. Tell 'im
yourself.

JOE

Eddie, I hate like hell for you to hear it this way. But when Vic
asked me how's business, well, you don't lie to a man who's just
done four years in the slammer for ya.

Eddie bobs his head up and down.

EDDIE

Oh really, is that a fact?

Eddie jumps Vic and they fall to the floor.

*The two friends, laughing and cussing at each other, wrestle on the floor
of Joe's office.*

Joe's on his feet yelling at them.

JOE
(yelling)

Okay, okay, enough, enough! Playtime's over! You wanna roll
around on the floor, do it in Eddie's office, not mine!

*The two men break it up. They are completely disheveled, hair a mess,
shirt-tails out. As they get themselves together, they continue to taunt one
another.*

EDDIE

Daddy, did ya see that?

JOE

What?

EDDIE

Guy got me on the ground, tried to fuck me.

VIC

You fuckin wish.

EDDIE

You tried to fuck me in my father's office, you sick bastard. Look, Vic, whatever you wanna do in the privacy of your own home, go to it. But don't try to fuck me. I don't think of you that way. I mean, I like you a lot –

VIC

Eddie, if I was a pirate, I wouldn't throw you to the crew.

EDDIE

No, you'd keep me, for yourself. Four years fuckin' punks in the ass made you appreciate prime rib when you get it.

VIC

I might break you, Nice Guy, but I'd make you my dog's bitch. You'd be suckin' the dick and going down on a mangy T-bone hound.

EDDIE

Now ain't that a sad sight, daddy, walks into jail a white man, walks out talkin' like a nigger. It's all that black semen been shootin' up his butt. It's backed up into his brain and comes out of his mouth.

VIC

Eddie, you keep talkin' like a bitch, I'm gonna slap you like a bitch.

JOE

Are you two finished? We were talkin' about some serious shit when you came in, Eddie. We got a big problem we're tryin' to solve. Now, Eddie, would you like to sit down and help us solve it, or do you two wanna piss fart around?

Playtime is over and Vic and Eddie know it. So they both take seats in front of Joe's desk.

Now Vic was tellin' me, he's got a parole problem.

EDDIE

Really? Who's your PO?

VIC

Seymour Scagnetti.

EDDIE

Scagnetti? Oh shit, I hear he's a motherfucker.

VIC

He is a fucker. He won't let me leave the halfway house till I get some piece of shit job.

EDDIE

You're coming back to work for us, right?

VIC

I wanna. But I gotta show this asshole I got an honest-to-goodness job before he'll let me move out on my own. I can't work for you guys and be worried about gettin' back before ten o'clock curfew.

JOE
(to Eddie)

We can work this out, can't we?

EDDIE

This isn't all that bad. We can give you a lot of legitimate jobs. Put you on the rotation at Long Beach as a dock worker.

VIC

I don't wanna lift crates.

EDDIE

You don't hafta lift shit. You don't really work there. But as far as the records are concerned, you do. I call up Matthews, the foreman, tell him he's got a new guy. Boom! You're on the schedule. You'll start getting a pay check at the end of the week. And ya know dock workers don't do too bad. So you can move into a halfway decent place without Scagnetti thinkin' 'What the fuck. Where's the money coming from?' And if Scagnetti ever wants to make a surprise visit, you're gone that day. That day we sent you to Tustin. 'Sorry, Scagnetti, we hadda bunch of shit out there we needed him to unload.' 'Tough luck, Seymour. You just missed him. We sent him to the Taft airstrip, five hours away, he's pickin' up a bunch of shit and bringing it back.' You see part of your job is goin' different places – and we got places all over the place.

JOE
(to Vic)

Didn't I tell ya not to worry?

(*To Eddie*)

Vic was worried.

EDDIE

Me and you'll drive down to Long Beach tomorrow. I'll introduce you to Matthews, tell him what's going on.

VIC

That's great, guy, thanks a bunch.

(*pause*)

When do you think you'll need me for real work.

JOE

Well, it's kinda a strange time right now. Things are kinda –

EDDIE

– Nuts. We got a big meeting in Vegas coming up. And we're kinda just gettin' ready for that right now.

JOE

Let Nice Guy set you up at Long Beach. Give ya some cash, get that Scagnetti fuck off your back, and we'll be talking to ya.

EDDIE

Daddy, I got an idea. Now just hear it out. I know you don't like to use any of the boys on these jobs, but technically Vic ain't one of the boys. He's been gone for four years. He ain't on no one's list. Ya know he can handle himself, ya know you can trust him.

Joe looks at Vic.

Vic has no idea what they're talking about.

JOE

How would you feel about pullin' a heist with about five other guys?

FADE TO BLACK:

INT. NICE GUY EDDIE'S CAR (MOVING) – DAY

Nice Guy Eddie is driving to the rendezvous talking on his portable car phone. The sounds of the seventies are coming out of his car radio in the form of 'Love Grows Where My Rosemary Goes' by Edison Lighthouse.

EDDIE
(*into phone*)

Hey Dov, we got a major situation here.

53

(*pause*)

I know you know that. I gotta talk with Daddy and find out what he wants done.

FLASH ON

INT. WAREHOUSE – DAY

The Cop is standing in the warehouse with his hands cuffed behind his back. Mr White, Mr Pink and Mr Blonde surround him and proceed to beat the shit out of him. 'Love Grows . . .' Plays over the soundtrack.

BACK TO NICE GUY EDDIE

EDDIE
(*into phone*)

All I know is what Vic told me. He said the place turned into a fuckin' bullet festival. He took a cop as hostage, just to get the fuck out of there.

FLASH ON

WAREHOUSE

The three men are stomping the cop into the ground.

BACK TO EDDIE

EDDIE
(*into phone*)

Do I sound like I'm jokin'? He's fuckin' driving around with the cop in his trunk.

(*pause*)

I don't know who did what. I don't know who has the loot, if anybody has the loot. Who's dead, who's alive, who's caught, who's not . . . I will know, I'm practically there. But what do I tell these guys about Daddy?

(*pause*)

Okay, that's what I'll tell em.

CUT TO:

EXT. WAREHOUSE – DAY

Three cars belonging to the other guys are parked outside the warehouse.

Eddie drives his car up to the warehouse. He gets out of the car, looks at the other cars parked outside.

>   EDDIE
>   (*to himself*)
> Fucking assholes.

Eddie makes a beeline for the front door, bangs it open, and steps inside the warehouse.

INT. WAREHOUSE – DAY

The robbers have the cop tied to a chair and are still wailing on him.

Nice Guy Eddie walks in and everybody jumps.

>   EDDIE
> What in Sam Hill is goin' on?

Mr Pink and Mr White speak together.

>   MR PINK
> Hey, Nice Guy, we got a cop.
>   WHITE
>   (*at the same time*)
> You're askin' what's goin' on? Where the fuck is Joe?

Nice Guy sees Mr Orange.

>   EDDIE
> Holy shit, Orange's all fucked up!
>   WHITE
> No shit, he's gonna fuckin' die on us if we don't get him taken
> care of.
>   MR PINK
> We were set up, the cops were waiting for us.
>   EDDIE
> What? Nobody set anybody up.
>   MR PINK
> The cops were there waitin' for us!

56

EDDIE

Bullshit.

MR PINK

Hey, fuck you, man, you weren't there, we were. And I'm tellin' ya, the cops had that store staked out.

EDDIE

Okay, Mr Detective, who did it?

MR PINK

What the fuck d'you think we've been askin' each other?

EDDIE

And what are your answers? Was it me? You think I set you up?

MR PINK

I don't know, but somebody did.

EDDIE

Nobody did. You cowboys turn the jewelry store into a wild west show, and you wonder why cops show up.

MR BLONDE

Where's Joseph?

EDDIE

I ain't talked to him. I talked to Dov. Dov said Daddy's comin' down here, and he's fucking pissed.

MR PINK
(*to Mr White*)

I told ya he'd be pissed.

MR BLONDE

What did Joe say?

EDDIE

I told you, I haven't talked to him. All I know is, he's pissed.

MR WHITE
(*pointing to Mr Orange*)

What are you gonna do about him?

EDDIE

Jesus Christ, give me a fuckin' chance to breathe. I got a few questions of my own, ya know.

MR WHITE

You ain't dying, he is.

EDDIE

I can see that, Mr Compassion. I'll call somebody.

MR WHITE

Who?

EDDIE

A snake charmer, what the fuck d'you think. I'll call a doctor,
he'll fix 'm right up. No, where's Mr Brown and Mr Blue?

MR PINK

Brown's dead, we don't know about Blue.

EDDIE

Fuck, man. They killed Brown? Are you sure?

MR WHITE

Yeah I'm fuckin' sure, I was there. He took it in the face and in
the neck.

EDDIE

And nobody's got a clue what happened to Mr Blue?

MR BLONDE

Well, he's either dead or he's alive or the cops got him or they
don't.

Dolly to medium on the cop.

EDDIE
(*off*)

I take it this is the bastard you told me about.
(*referring to the cop*)
Why the hell are you beating the shit out of him?

MR PINK

So he'll tell us who the fuck set us up.

EDDIE

Would you stop it with that shit! You beat on this prick enough,
he'll tell ya he started the Chicago fire. That don't necessarily
make it so. Okay, first things fucking last, where's the shit? Please
tell me somebody brought something with them.

MR PINK

I got a bag. I stashed it till I could be sure this place wasn't a police
station.

EDDIE

Good for you. Well, let's go get it. We also gotta get rid of all those
cars. It looks like Sam's hot car lot outside.
(*pointing to Mr Blonde*)
You stay here and babysit Orange and the cop.

58

(referring to Mr Pink and Mr White)

You two take a car each, I'll follow ya. You ditch it, I'll pick you up, then we'll pick up the stones. And while I'm following you, I'll arrange for some sort of a doctor for our friend.

MR WHITE

We can't leave these guys with him.

(meaning Mr Blonde)

EDDIE

Why not?

Mr White crosses to Mr Blonde.

MR WHITE

Because this guy's a fucking psycho. And if you think Joe's pissed at us, that ain't nothing compared to how pissed off I am at him, for puttin' me in the same room as this bastard.

MR BLONDE

(to Eddie)

You see what I been puttin' up with? As soon as I walk through the door I'm hit with this shit. I tell 'em what you told me about us stayin' put and Mr White whips out his gun, sticks it in my face, and starts screaming, 'You motherfucker, I'm gonna blow you away, blah, blah, blah.'

MR WHITE

He's the reason the place turned into a shooting gallery.

(to Mr Pink)

What are you, a silent partner? Fuckin' tell him.

MR PINK

He seems all right now, but he went crazy in the store.

MR WHITE

This is what he was doin'.

Mr White acts out Mr Blonde shooting everybody in the store.

MR BLONDE

I told 'em not to touch the alarm. They touched it. I blew 'em full of holes. If they hadn't done what I told 'em not to, they'd still be alive today.

MR WHITE

That's your excuse for going on a kill crazy rampage?

59

MR BLONDE

I don't like alarms.

EDDIE

What does it matter who stays with the cop? We ain't lettin' him
go. Not after he's seen everybody. You should've never took him
outta your trunk in the first place.

MR PINK

We were trying to find out what he knew about the set up.

EDDIE

There is no fuckin' set up!

(*Eddie takes charge*)

Look, this is the news. Blondie, you stay here and take care of
them two. White and Pink come with me, 'cuz if Joe gets here and
sees all those fucking cars parked out front, he's going to be as
mad at me as he is at you.

*Eddie, Mr White and Mr Pink walk out of the warehouse talking
amongst themselves.*

INT. WAREHOUSE – DAY – MR BLONDE AND COP

*Mr Blonde closes the door after them. He then slowly turns his head
towards the cop.*

MR BLONDE

CU – COP'S FACE.

MR BLONDE
(*off*)

Now where were we?

COP

I told you I don't know anything about any fucking set up. I've
only been on the force eight months, nobody tells me anything! I
don't know anything! You can torture me if you want –

MR BLONDE
(*off*)

Thanks, don't mind if I do.

COP

Your boss even said there wasn't a set up.

MR BLONDE
(off)

First off, I don't have a boss. Are you clear about that?

He slaps the cop's face.

MR BLONDE
(off)

I asked you a question. Are you clear about that?

COP

Yes.

MR BLONDE
(off)

Now I'm not gonna bullshit you. I don't really care about what you know or don't know. I'm gonna torture you for a while regardless. Not to get information, but because torturing a cop amuses me. There's nothing you can say, I've heard it all before. There's nothing you can do. Except pray for a quick death, which you ain't gonna get.

He puts a piece of tape over the cop's mouth.

COP'S POV

Mr Blonde walks away from the cop.

MR BLONDE

Let's see what's on K-Billy's 'super sounds of the seventies' weekend.

He turns on the radio.

Stealer's Wheel's hit 'Stuck in the Middle with You' plays out the speaker.

Note: This entire sequence is timed to the music.

Mr Blonde slowly walks toward the cop. He opens a large knife.†

*[He grabs a chair, places it in front of the cop and sits on it.]

Mr Blonde just stares into the cop's/our face, holding the knife, singing along with the song.

Then, like a cobra, he lashes out.

† Razor in completed film.
* Cut from completed film.

A slash across the face.

The cop/camera moves around wildly.

Mr Blonde just stares into the cop's/our face, singing along with the seventies hit.

Then he reaches out and cuts off the cop's/our ear.

The cop/camera moves around wildly.

Mr Blonde holds the ear up to the cop/us to see.

*[Mr Blonde rises, kicking the chair he was sitting on out of the way.]

INT./EXT. WAREHOUSE – DAY – HANDHELD SHOT

We follow Mr Blonde as he walks out of the warehouse . . . to his car. He opens the trunk, pulls out a large can of gasoline.

He walks back inside the warehouse . . .

INT. WAREHOUSE – DAY

. . . carrying the can of gas.

Mr Blonde pours the gasoline all over the cop, who's begging him not to do this.

Mr Blonde just sings along with Stealer's Wheel.

Mr Blonde lights up a match and, while mouthing:

MR BLONDE
'Clowns to the left of me, jokers to the right. Here I am, stuck in the middle with you.'

He moves the match up to the cop . . .

. . . When a bullet explodes in Mr Blonde's chest.

The handheld camera whips to the right and we see the bloody Mr Orange firing his gun.

We cut back and forth between Mr Blonde taking bullet hits and Mr Orange emptying his weapon.

* Cut from completed film.

63

Mr Blonde falls down dead.

Mr Orange crawls to where the cop is, leaving a bloody trail behind him.
When he reaches the cop's feet he looks up at him.

> MR ORANGE
> (*feebly*)

What's your name?

> COP

Marvin.

> MR ORANGE

Marvin what?

> COP

Marvin Nash.

> MR ORANGE

Listen to me, Marvin Nash. I'm a cop.

> MARVIN

I know.

> MR ORANGE
> (*surprised*)

You do?

> MARVIN

Your name's Freddy something.

> MR ORANGE

Freddy Newendyke.

> MARVIN

Frankie Ferchetti introduced us once, about five months ago.

> MR ORANGE

Shit. I don't remember that at all.

> MARVIN

I do.

> (*pause*)

How do I look?

The gut-shot Mr Orange looks at the kid's gashed face and the hole in the
side of his head where his ear use to be.

> MR ORANGE

I don't know what to tell you, Marvin.

Marvin starts to weep.

That fucking bastard! That fucking sick fucking bastard!

Marvin, I need you to hold on. There's officers positioned and waiting to move in a block away.

MARVIN
(*screaming*)
What the fuck are they waiting for? That motherfucker cut off my ear! He slashed my face! I'm deformed!

MR ORANGE
And I'm dying. They don't know that. All they know is they're not to make a move until Joe Cabot shows up. I was sent undercover to get Cabot. You heard 'em, they said he's on his way. Don't pussy out on me now, Marvin. We're just gonna sit here and bleed until Joe Cabot sticks his fuckin' head through that door.

CUT TO:

TITLE CARD:

'MR ORANGE'

INT. DENNY'S – NIGHT

A tough-looking black man named Holdaway, who sports a Malcolm X beard, a green Chairman Mao cap with a red star on it, and a military flack jacket, digs into a Denny bacon, cheese and avocado burger. He sits in a booth all alone. He's waiting for somebody. As he waits, he practically empties an entire bottle of ketchup on his french fries, not by mistake either – that's just how he likes it.

We see Mr Orange, now known as Freddy Newendyke, wearing a high school letterman jacket, enter the coffee shop, spot Holdaway, and head his way. Holdaway sees Freddy bop towards him with a wide-ass alligator grin plastered across his face.

Camera dollies fast down aisle to medium shot of Holdaway. We hear Freddy off screen.

FREDDY
(*off*)

Say 'hello' to a motherfucker who's inside. Cabot's doing a job and take a big fat guess who he wants on the team?

HOLDAWAY

This better not be some Freddy joke.

LOW ANGLE
looking up at Freddy, who's standing at the table.

FREDDY

It ain't no joke, I'm in there. I'm up his ass.

CU – HOLDAWAY
Holdaway just looks at his pupil for a moment, then smiles.

HOLDAWAY

Congratulations.

EXT. DENNY – NIGHT

Through the window of the restaurant we see Freddy slide into the booth across from Holdaway. Freddy's doing a lot of talking, but we can't hear what they're saying.

INT. DENNY – NIGHT
FREEZE FRAME ON HOLDAWAY

We are frozen on a medium close up of Holdaway listening to Freddy. We hear restaurant noise and Freddy off screen.

FREDDY
(*off*)

Nice Guy Eddie tells me Joe wants to meet me. He says I should just hang around my apartment and wait for a phone call. Well, after waiting three goddamn days by the fuckin' phone, he calls me last night and says Joe's ready, and he'll pick me up in fifteen minutes.

The freeze frame ends. Holdaway comes suddenly up to speed and says:

HOLDAWAY

Who all picked you up?

From here to end we cut back and forth.

FREDDY

Nice Guy. When we got to the bar . . .

HOLDAWAY

. . . What bar?

FREDDY

The Boots and Socks in Gardena. When we got there, I met Joe and a guy named Mr White. It's a phony name. My name's Mr Orange.

HOLDAWAY

You ever seen this motherfucker before?

FREDDY

Who, Mr White?

HOLDAWAY

Yeah.

FREDDY

No, he ain't familiar. He ain't one of Cabot's soldiers either. He's gotta be from outta town. But Joe knows him real well.

HOLDAWAY

How can you tell?

FREDDY

The way they talk to each other. You can tell they're buddies.

HOLDAWAY

Did the two of you talk?

FREDDY

Me and Mr White?

HOLDAWAY

Yeah.

FREDDY

A little.

HOLDAWAY

What about?

FREDDY

The Brewers.

HOLDAWAY

The Milwaukee Brewers?

FREDDY

Yeah. They had just won the night before, and he made a killing off 'em.

HOLDAWAY

Well, if this crook's a Brewers fan, his ass has gotta be from
Wisconsin. And I'll bet you everything from a diddle-eyed Joe to a
damned-if-I-know, that in Milwaukee they got a sheet on this Mr
White motherfucker's ass. I want you to go through the mugs of
guys from old Milwaukee with a history of armed robbery, and
put a name to that face.

Holdaway takes a big bite out of his burger.

(*with his mouth full*)
What kinda questions did Cabot ask?

FREDDY

Where I was from, who I knew, how I knew Nice Guy, had I done
time, shit like that.

*Holdaway's talked enough, he's eating his burger now. He motions for
Freddy to elaborate.*

He asked me if I ever done armed robbery before. I read him my
credits. I robbed a few gas and sips, sold some weed, told him
recently I held the shotgun while me and another guy pulled down
a poker game in Portland.

HOLDAWAY

How was Long Beach Mike's referal?

FREDDY

Perfecto! His backin' me up went a long fuckin' way. I told 'em it
was Long Beach Mike I did the poker game with. When Nice Guy
called him to check it out, he said I was A-okay. He told 'em I was
a good thief, I didn't rattle, and I was ready to make a move. What
happens to Long Beach Mike now?

HOLDAWAY

We'll take care of him.

FREDDY

Do right by him, he's a good guy. I wouldn't be inside if it wasn't
for him.

HOLDAWAY

Long Beach Mike isn't your amigo, he's a fuckin' scumbag. The
piece of shit is selling out his real amigos, that's how much of a
good fuckin' guy he is. We'll look after his ass, but get that no
good motherfucker outta mind, and tend to business.

Camera moves from a medium on Freddy to a closeup.

> HOLDAWAY
> (*off*)
>
> Didja use the commode story?

> FREDDY
>
> Fuckin'-A. I tell it real good, too.

EXT. ROOFTOP — DAY

Freddy and Holdaway at one of their many rendezvous, an LA city rooftop.

> FREDDY
>
> What's this?

> HOLDAWAY
>
> It's a scene. Memorize it.

> FREDDY
>
> What?

> HOLDAWAY
>
> An undercover cop has got to be Marlon Brando. To do this job you got to be a great actor. You got to be naturalistic. You got to

be naturalistic as hell. If you ain't a great actor you're a bad actor, and bad acting is bullshit in this job.

FREDDY
(referring to the papers)

But what is this?

HOLDAWAY

It's an amusing anecdote about a drug deal.

FREDDY

What?

HOLDAWAY

Some funny shit that happened while you were doing a job.

FREDDY

I gotta memorize all this? There's over four fuckin' pages of shit here.

HOLDAWAY

It's like a fuckin' joke, man. You remember what's important and the rest you make your own. You can tell a joke, can't ya?

FREDDY

I can tell a joke.

HOLDAWAY

Well just think about it like that. Now the things you hafta remember are the details. It's the details that sell your story. Now your story takes place in a men's room. So you gotta know the details about that men's room. You gotta know if they got paper towels or a blower to dry your hands. You gotta know if the stalls got doors or not. You gotta know if they got liquid soap or that pink granulated powder shit. If they got hot water or not. If it stinks. If some nasty motherfucker sprayed diarrhea all over one of the bowls. You gotta know every damn thing there is to know about that commode. And the people in your story, you gotta know the details about them, too. Anybody can tell who did what to whom. But in real life, when people tell a story, they try to recreate the event in the other person's mind. Now what you gotta do is take all them details and make 'em your own. This story's gotta be about you, and how you perceived the events that took place. And the way you make it your own is you just gotta keep sayin' it and sayin' it and sayin' it and sayin' it and sayin' it.

71

Freddy paces back and forth, in and out of frame, rehearsing the anecdote. He's reading it pretty good, but he's still reading it from the page, and every once in a while he stumbles over his words.

FREDDY
. . . this was during the Los Angeles marijuana drought of '86. I still had a connection. Which was insane, 'cause you couldn't get weed anyfuckinwhere then. Anyway, I had a connection with this hippie chick up in Santa Cruz. And all my friends knew it. And they'd give me a call and say, 'Hey, Freddy, you buyin' some, you think you could buy me some too?' They knew I smoked, so they'd ask me to buy a little for them when I was buyin'. But it got to be everytime I bought some weed, I was buyin' for four or five different people. Finally I said, 'Fuck this shit.' I'm makin' this bitch rich. She didn't have to do jack shit, she never even had to meet these people. I was fuckin' doin' all the work. So I got together with her and told her, 'Hey, I'm sick of this shit. I'm comin' through for everybody, and nobody's comin' through for me. So, either I'm gonna tell all my friends to find their own source, or you give me a bunch of weed, I'll sell it to them, give you the money, minus ten percent, and I get my pot for free.' So, I did it for a while . . .

Freddy exits frame.

CUT TO:

EXT. ROOFTOP — DAY

Another empty frame, except obviously outside. Freddy enters frame from the same direction he exited in the previous scene, finishing his sentence. When we move to a wider shot we see Freddy performing his monologue to Holdaway. Freddy paces back and forth as he performs his story.

FREDDY
. . . but then that got to be a pain in the ass. People called me on the phone all the fuckin' time. I couldn't rent a fuckin' tape without six phone calls interrupting me. 'Hey, Freddy when's the next time you're gettin' some?' 'Motherfucker, I'm tryin' to watch *Lost Boys* – when I have some, I'll let you know.' And then these

rinky-dink pot heads come by – they're my friends and everything, but still. I got all my shit laid out in sixty dollar bags. Well, they don't want sixty dollars worth. They want ten dollars worth. Breaking it up is a major fuckin' pain in the ass. I don't even know how much ten dollars worth is. 'Well, fuck, man, I don't want that much around. If I have that much around I'll smoke it.' 'Hey, if you guys can't control your smokin', that's not my problem. You motherfuckers been smokin' for five years, be adult about it.' Finally I just told my connection, count me out. But as it turns out, I'm the best guy she had, and she depended alot on my business. But I was still sick to death of it. And she's tryin' to talk me into not quitin'.

Now this was a very weird situation, 'cause I don't know if you remember back in '86 there was a major fuckin' drought. Nobody had anything. People were livin' on resin and smokin' the wood in their pipes for months. And this chick had a bunch, and was beggin' me to sell it. So I told her I wasn't gonna be Joe the Pot Man anymore. But I would take a little bit and sell it to my close, close, close friends. She agreed to that, and said we'd keep the same arrangement as before, ten percent and free pot for me, as long as I helped her out that weekend. She had a brick of weed she was sellin', and she didn't want to go to the buy alone.

CUT TO:

INT. BOOTS AND SOCKS BAR – NIGHT

Freddy, Joe, Nice Guy Eddie and Mr White all sit around a table in a red-lighted smokey bar. Freddy continues his story. The crooks are enjoying the hell out of it.

FREDDY

. . . Her brother usually goes with her, but he's in county unexpectedly.

MR WHITE

What for?

FREDDY

Traffic tickets gone to warrant. They stopped him for something, found the warrants on 'im, took 'im to jail. She doesn't want to walk around alone with all that weed. Well, I don't wanna do this,

73

I have a bad feeling about it, but she keeps askin' me, keeps askin' me, finally I said okay 'cause I'm sick of listening to it. Well, we're picking this guy up at the train station.

JOE

You're picking the buyer up at the train station? You're carrying the weed on you?

FREDDY

Yeah, the guy needed it right away. Don't ask me why. So we get to the train station, and we're waitin' for the guy. Now I'm carrying the weed in one of those carry-on bags, and I gotta take a piss. So I tell the connection I'll be right back, I'm goin' to the little boys room . . .

CUT TO:

INT. MEN'S ROOM – TRAIN STATION – DAY

MEDIUM ON FREDDY
He walks through the door with a carry-on bag over his shoulder. Once he's inside, he stops in his tracks. We move into a closeup.

FREDDY
(*voice over*)
. . . So I walk into the men's room, and who's standing there?

FREEZE FRAME
on Freddy standing in front of four Los Angeles County Sheriffs and one German Shepherd. All of their eyes are on Freddy. Everyone is frozen.

FREDDY
(*voice over*)
. . . four Los Angeles County Sheriffs and a German Shepherd.

NICE GUY EDDIE
(*voice over*)
They were waitin' for you?

FREDDY
(*voice over*)
No. They were just a bunch of cops hangin' out in the men's room, talkin'. When I walked through the door they all stopped what they were talking about and looked at me.

74

BACK TO BAR

EXTREME CU – MR WHITE

> MR WHITE
> That's hard, man. That's a fuckin' hard situation.

BACK TO MEN'S ROOM

EXTREME CU GERMAN SHEPHERD

barking his head off.

> FREDDY
> (*voice over*)
> The German Shepherd starts barkin'. He's barkin' at me. I mean it's obvious he's barkin' at me.

We do a slow 360 around Freddy in the men's room. We can hear the dog barking.

> Every nerve ending, all of my senses, the blood in my veins, everything I had was screaming, 'Take off, man, just take off, get the fuck outta there!' Panic hit me like a bucket of water. First there was the shock of it – BAM, right in the face! Then I'm just stanin' there drenched in panic.

> And all those sheriffs are lookin' at me and they know. They can smell it. As sure as that fuckin' dog can, they can smell it on me.

FREEZE FRAME
Freeze frame shot of Freddy standing in front of the sheriffs. It suddenly jerks to life, and moves to speed. The dog is barking. Freddy moves to his right, out of frame. We stay on the sheriffs. One sheriff yells at the dog.

> SHERIFF #1
> Shut up!

The dog quietens down. Sheriff #2 continues with his story. A couple of the sheriffs look over at Freddy off screen, but as Sheriff #2 talks, turn their attention to him.

So my gun's drawn, right? I got it aimed right at him. I tell 'im, 'Freeze, don't fuckin' move.' And the little idiot's lookin' at me, nodding his head 'Yes,' sayin', 'I know . . . I know . . . I know.' Meanwhile, his right hand is creepin' towards his glove box. So I scream at him, 'Asshole, you better fuckin' freeze right now!' And he's still lookin' at me, saying 'I know . . . I know . . . I know.' And his right hand's still going for the glove box.

The camera pans away from the sheriffs to Freddy, up against the urinal, playing possum, pretending to piss.

I tell 'im, 'Buddy, I'm gonna shoot you in the face right now if you don't put your hands on the fuckin' dash.' And the guy's girlfriend, a real sexy Oriental bitch, starts screamin' at him, 'Chuck, are you out of your mind? Put your hands on the dash like the officer said.' And then like nothing, the guy snaps out of it and casually puts his hands on the dash.

Freddy finishes his playing possum piss, and walks past the sheriffs over to the sink. The camera pans with him. A sheriff is sitting on a sink. He looks down and watches Freddy wash his hands.

SHERIFF #1

What was he goin' for?

SHERIFF #2

His registration. Stupid fuckin' citizen, doesn't have the slightest idea how close he came to gettin' shot.

Freddy finishes washing his hands. He goes to dry them, but there's only those hand drying machines. Freddy turns on the drying machine. He can't hear anything the sheriffs say now. The sound of the machine dominates the sound track.

These following shots are slow motion.

CU – FREDDY
CU – *his hands, rubbing each other getting blown dry.*

Shot of Sheriffs staring at Freddy.

CU – FREDDY

CU – FREDDY'S HANDS.

CU – GERMAN SHEPHERD

He barks. We can't hear him because of the machine. Machine turns off. Freddy turns and walks out of the room.

BACK TO BAR

CU – JOE

> JOE
> (*laughing*)
> That's how you do it, kid. You knew how to handle that situation. You shit your pants, and then you just dive in and swim.

In slow motion Joe lights a cigar.

> HOLDAWAY
> (*off*)
> Tell me more about Cabot.

> FREDDY
> (*off*)
> He's a cool guy. A real nice, real funny, real cool guy.

CUT TO:

**[INT. DENNY'S – NIGHT

> FREDDY
> You remember *The Fantastic Four?*

> HOLLOWAY
> Yeah.

> FREDDY
> The Thing. The motherfucker looks just like The Thing.]

*[CUT TO:

INT. FREDDY'S APARTMENT – DAY

Freddy is sitting at a table, eating Captain Crunch, and flipping through mug shots.

** Added during shooting.
* Cut from completed film.

78

CU – SOME UGLY MUGS

Then we come to Mr White's mug shot.

Freddy's recognition.

He grabs his phone, dials a number, and takes a quick spoonful of cereal before it's answered.

> HOLDAWAY
> (*off*)
>
> Whatcha want?

> FREDDY
> (*mouthful*)
>
> Jim?

> HOLDAWAY
> (*off*)
>
> Who the fuck is this?

He swallows.

> FREDDY
>
> Freddy Newendyke.

> HOLDAWAY
> (*off*)
>
> You find him yet, Newendyke?

79

                    FREDDY
I'm lookin' at him right now.
                    HOLDAWAY
                     (off)
So what's Mr White's real name?
                    FREDDY
Lawrence Dimick, D-I-M-I-C-K.
                    HOLDAWAY
                     (off)
Good work, Newendyke. We'll see what we can find out about Mr
Dimick's ass.

CUT TO:

INT. COMPUTER ROOM – DAY

CU – COMPUTER SCREEN

the name Dimick, Lawrence is typed in.

CU – ENTER BUTTON IS PUNCHED

CU – FEMALE COMPUTER OPERATOR, JODIE McCLUSKEY

                    JODIE
This is your life, Lawrence Dimick!

CU – COMPUTER PRINTER

*printing out sheet. The noise of the printer plays loud over the soundtrack.
Jodie's hand comes into frame and tears sheet from the printer.*

CUT TO:

EXT. HAMBURGER STAND – DAY

*Freddy, Holdaway, and Jodie sit at a cabana table in front of a humburger
stand, stuffing their faces with gigantic burgers.*

                    HOLDAWAY
Read us what you got, McCluskey.
                    JODIE
Lawrence 'Larry' Dimick. Also known as Lawrence Jacobs and
Alvin 'Al' Jacobs. This guy is Mr Joe-Armed-Robbery. He's a pro

and he makes it a habit not to get caught. He's only been convicted
twice, which is pretty good for somebody living a life of crime.
Once for armed robbery, when he was twenty-one, in Milwaukee.

FREDDY

What was it?

JODIE

Payroll office at a lumber yard. First offense – he got eighteen
months. He didn't get busted again until he was thirty-two. And
then it was a backdoor bust. A routine vice squad roust. They roust
this bar, our buddy Lawrence is in there knocking down a few. He
gets picked up. He's wearing on his person an outlaw .45
automatic, apparently his weapon of choice. Also, on his finger is a
diamond ring from a jewelry store robbery a year earlier. He got two
years back inside for that.

Freddy winces.

FREDDY

Goddamn, that's hard time.

JODIE

So far, it's the only time he's ever done.

HOLDAWAY

Was this vice squad bullshit in Milwaukee?

JODIE

No. The vice squad roust was in LA. He's been in Los Angeles
since '77.

FREDDY

When did he do this time?

JODIE

Back in '83, got out late '86. I found something else out I think you
two should be aware of. About a year and a half ago, up in
Sacramento, an undercover cop, John Dolenz, worked his way into
a bank job. Apparently before the job they found out he was a cop.
Now picture this: it's Dolenz's birthday, a bunch of cops are
waiting in his apartment for a surprise party. The door opens,
everyone yells 'Surprise!', and standing in the doorway is Dolenz
and this other guy sticking a gun in Dolenz ribs. Before anybody
knows what's going on, this stranger shoots Dolenz dead and starts
firing two .45 automatics into the crowd.

HOLDAWAY

What happened?

JODIE

It was a mess. Cops got hit, wives got hit, girlfriends got hit, his dog got hit. People got glass in their faces. Three were killed, six were wounded.

FREDDY

They couldn't pin the killing on one of the bank robbers?

JODIE

They tried, but they didn't have a positive ID and all those guys had alibis. Besides, we really didn't have anything on them. We had the testimony of a dead man that they were talking about committing a robbery. They never went ahead with the bank job.

FREDDY

And Larry Dimick was one of the boys?

JODIE

He was probably the one.

HOLDAWAY

Just how sure are you with your cover?

FREDDY

Today they may know something, tomorrow they may know something else, but yesterday they didn't know anything. What's the next step.

HOLDAWAY

Do what they told ya. Sit in your apartment and wait for 'em to call you. We'll have guys posted outside who'll follow you when they pick you up.]

INT. FREDDY'S – DAY

CU – TELEPHONE
It rings. Freddy answers it, we follow the receiver up to his face.

FREDDY

Hello.

NICE GUY EDDIE
(*off – through phone*)
It's showtime. Grab your jacket –

INT. NICE GUY EDDIE'S CAR (PARKED) – DAY

CU – *Nice Guy Eddie speaking into the car phone*

> EDDIE
> – We're parked outside.

> FREDDY
> (*off – through phone*)
> I'll be right down.

Through the phone we hear the click of Freddy hanging up. Nice Guy places the receiver back in its cradle.

> EDDIE
> He'll be right down.

INT. FREDDY'S APARTMENT – DAY

The camera follows Freddy as he hops around the apartment getting everything he needs. He puts on his jacket and slips on some sneakers.

Before he goes he roots around among some coins on the table, finds his ring and puts it on.

*Dolly fast toward the front door knob. Freddy's hand comes into frame,
grabs the knob, then lets go. We move up to his face.*

FREDDY
(*to himself*)

Don't pussy out on me now. They don't know. They don't know shit.
(*pause*)

You're not gonna get hurt. You're fucking Baretta and they believe
every word, cuz you're super cool.

He exits frame. We stay put and hear the door open and close off screen.

EXT. FREDDIE'S APARTMENT – DAY

COPS' POV

*From inside an unmarked car across the street, the two cops watching
Freddy see him walk out of his building and up to Eddie's parked car.*

COP #1
(*off*)

There goes our boy.

COP #2
(*off*)

I swear, a guy has to have rocks in his head the size of Gibraltar to
work undercover.

COP #1
(*off*)

Do you want one of these?

COP #2
(*off*)

Yeah, gimme the bear claw.

*Freddy gets into the car and it pulls into traffic. Cop #1 starts the engine
and follows.*

INT. NICE GUY EDDIE'S CAR (MOVING) – DAY

*Nice Guy Eddie is behind the wheel. Mr Pink is in the passenger seat.
Freddy and Mr White are in the backseat together.*

MR PINK

. . . Hey, I know what I'm talkin' about, black women ain't the
same as white women.

MR WHITE
(*sarcastically*)

There's a slight difference.

The car laughs.

MR PINK

Go ahead and laugh, you know what I mean. What a white bitch
will put up with, a black bitch won't put up with for a minute. They
got a line, and if you cross it, they fuck you up.

EDDIE

I gotta go along with Mr Pink on this. I've seen it happen.

MR WHITE

Okay, Mr Expert. If this is such a truism, how come every nigger I
know treats his woman like a piece of shit?

MR PINK

I'll make you a bet that those same damn niggers who were showin'
their ass in public, when their bitches get 'em home, they chill the
fuck out.

MR WHITE

Not these guys.

MR PINK

Yeah, those guys too.

EDDIE

Let me tell you guys a story. In one of Daddy's clubs there was this
black cocktail waitress named Elois.

MR WHITE

Elois?

EDDIE

Yeah, Elois. E and Lois. We called her Lady E.

MR WHITE

Where was she from, Compton?

No. She was from Ladora Heights.

MR PINK

The black Beverly Hills. I knew this lady from Ladora Heights
once.
                    (*in a stuck up black female voice*)
'Hi, I'm from Ladora Heights, it's the black Beverly Hills.'

EDDIE

It's not the black Beverly Hills, it's the black Palos Verdes.
Anyway, this chick, Elois, was a man-eater-upper. I bet every guy
who's ever met her has jacked off to her at least once. You know
who she looked like? Christie Love. 'Member that TV show *Get
Christie Love*? She was a black female cop. She always used to say,
'You're under arrest, sugar.'

MR PINK

I was in the sixth grade when that show was on. I totally dug it.
What the fuck was the name of the chick who played Christie Love?

EDDIE

Pam Grier.

MR PINK

No, it wasn't Pam Grier, Pam Grier was the other one. Pam Grier
made the movies. *Christie Love* was like a Pam Grier TV show,
without Pam Grier.

MR PINK

What the fuck was that chick's name? Oh this is just great, I'm
totally fuckin' tortured now.

EDDIE

Well, whoever she was, Elois looked like her. So one night I walk
into the club, and no Elois. Now the bartender was a wetback, he
was a friend of mine, his name was Carlos. So I asked him, 'Hey,
Carlos, where's Lady E tonight?' Well apparently Lady E was
married to this real piece of dog shit. I mean, a real animal. And
apparently he would do things to her.

FREDDY

Do things? What would he do? You mean like beat her up?

EDDIE

Nobody knows for sure what he did. We just knew he did
something. Anyway, Elois plays it real cool. And waits for the next
time this bag of shit gets drunk. So one night the guy gets drunk and
passes out on the couch. So while the guy's inebriated, she strips
him naked. Then she takes some crazy glue and glues his dick to his
belly.

The car reacts to how horrible that would be.

I'm dead fuckin' serious. She put some on his dick and some on his
belly, then stuck 'em together. The paramedics had to come and cut
it loose.

The car reacts badly.

MR WHITE

Jesus Christ!

FREDDY

You can do some crazy things with it.

EDDIE

I don't know what he did to her, but she got even.

MR WHITE

Was he all pissed off?

MR PINK

How would you feel if you had to do a handstand every time you
took a piss.

The car laughs.

*[EXT. WAREHOUSE – DAY

*Nice Guy Eddie pulls up outside the warehouse. The four men climb out of
the car and follow Eddie inside.*

INT. WAREHOUSE – DAY

The four men enter the building.

* Cut from completed film.

At the other end of the warehouse, sitting in chairs, are Mr Blonde, Mr Brown, Mr Blue and Joe Cabot.

We shoot this from overhead, looking down on the men.

> JOE
> *(to everybody)*

. . . So they're talkin about how they get their wives off, and the French guy says:

> *(in a bad French accent)*

'All I gotta do is take my pinky and tickle my Fifi's little oo-la-la and she rises a foot off the bed.'

Back to Joe.

So the dago says:

CU – JOE

> *(in a good Brooklyn accent)*

'That's nothin'. When I take the tip of my tongue and wiggle it against my Mary Louise's little fun pimple, she rises two feet off da bed.' Then our friend from Poland says:

> *(in a dumb voice)*

'You guys ain't no cocksmen. When I get through fuckin' my Sophie, I wipe my dick on the curtains and you know what? She hits the roof!'

Joe laughs like a crazy man.

Ha, ha, ha, ha, ha, ha!

We hear a lot of laughing off screen.

Ain't that a masterpiece? Stupid fuckin' Polack, wipes his dick on the drapes.

Joe's eyes greet the new arrivals.

You're here, great!

JOE EXITS – CU

We now have everybody from the Uncle Bob's Pancake House scene together again. The men sit on folding chairs, some stand. Joe sits in front of them on the edge of a table. A blackboard with a layout of the jewelry store is off to the right.

We do a 360 around the men.

EDDIE

We woulda gotten here sooner, but we got backed up around La Brea and Pico.

JOE

No hurry.
                    (*to the boys*)
All right, let's get to know one another.]

**[INT. WAREHOUSE – DAY

JOE

You guys like to tell jokes and giggle and kid around, huh? Giggling like a bunch of young broads in a school yard. Well, let me tell a joke.

Camera tracks across the men's faces.

Five guys sitting in a bull pen, San Quentin. Wondering how the fuck they got there. What'd we do wrong? What should we've done? What didn't we do? It's your fault, my fault, his fault. All that bullshit. Finally, someone comes up with the idea, wait a minute, while we were planning this caper, all we did was sit around and tell fucking jokes. Got the message? When this caper's over, and I'm sure it's gonna be a successful one, hell, we'll go down to the Hawaiian Islands and I'll roar and laugh with all of you. You'll find me a different character down there. Right now it's a matter of business.] With the exception of Eddie and myself, who you already know, you'll be using aliases. Under no circumstances are you to tell one another your real name or anything else about yourself. That includes where you're from, your wife's name, where you might've done time, about a bank in St Petersburg you might've robbed. You guys don't say shit about who you are, where you been or what you've done. Only thing you guys can talk about is what you're going to do. This way the only ones who know who the members of the team are are Eddie and myself. And that's the way I like it. Because in the unlikely event of one of you getting apprehended by the cops, not that I expect

** Added during shooting.

that to happen – it most definitely should not happen – it hasn't happened, you don't have anything to deal with. You don't know any names. You know my name, you know Eddie's name. That I don't care about. You gotta prove it. I ain't worried. Besides, this way you gotta trust me. I like that. I set this up and picked the men I wanted for it. None of you came to me, I approached all of you. I know you. I know your work, I know your reputation. I know you as men. Except for this guy.

Joe points a finger at Freddy.

Freddy shits a brick.

But he's OK. If he wasn't OK, he wouldn't be here. Okay, let me introduce everybody to everybody. But once again, at the risk of being redundant, if I even think I hear somebody telling or referring to somebody by their Christian name . . .
> (*Joe searches for the right words*)
. . . you won't want to be you. Okay, quickly.
> (*pointing at the men as he gives them a name*)
Mr Brown, Mr White, Mr Blonde, Mr Blue, Mr Orange, and Mr Pink.

MR PINK

Why am I Mr Pink?

JOE

'Cause you're a faggot.
Everybody laughs.

MR PINK

Why can't we pick out our own color?

JOE

I tried that once, it don't work. You get four guys fighting over who's gonna be Mr Black. Since nobody knows anybody else, nobody wants to back down. So forget it, I pick. Be thankful you're not Mr Yellow.

MR BROWN

Yeah, but Mr Brown? That's too close to Mr Shit.

Everybody laughs.

MR PINK

Yeah, Mr Pink sounds like Mr Pussy. Tell you what, let me be Mr Purple. That sounds good to me, I'm Mr Purple.

JOE

You're not Mr Purple, somebody from another job's Mr Purple. You're Mr Pink.

MR WHITE

Who cares what your name is? Who cares if you're Mr Pink, Mr Purple, Mr Pussy, Mr Piss . . .

MR PINK

Oh that's really easy for you to say, you're Mr White. You gotta cool-sounding name. So tell me, Mr White, if you think 'Mr Pink' is no big deal, you wanna trade?

JOE

Nobody's trading with anybody! Look, this ain't a goddamn fuckin' city council meeting! Listen up Mr Pink. We got two ways here, my way or the highway. And you can go down either of 'em. So what's it gonna be, Mr Pink?

MR PINK

Jesus Christ, Joe. Fuckin' forget it. This is beneath me. I'm Mr Pink, let's move on.

Camera leaves the team and goes to the blackboard with the layout of the jewelry store on it.

*[JOE
(*off*)

Okay, fellas, let's get into this.]

CUT TO:

**[JOE

I'll move on when I feel like it. All you guys got the goddamn message? I'm so goddamn mad I can hardly talk. Let's go to work.

Joe turns towards the blackboard.]

* Cut from completed film.
** Added during shooting.

Freddy and Holdaway sit on some bleachers in an empty little league baseball field.

HOLDAWAY

Okay, we're gonna station men across the street from Karina's Fine Jewelry. But their orders will be not to move in unless the robbery gets out of control. You gotta make sure they don't have to move in. You're inside to make sure that everything goes according to Hoyle. We have men set up a block away from the warehouse rendezvous. They got complete visibility of the exterior. So as soon as Joe Cabot shows up, we'll see it.

FREDDY

What's your visibility of the interior?

HOLDAWAY

We can't see shit on the inside. And we can't risk gettin' any closer for fear they'll spot us.

FREDDY

This is bullshit, Jim. I get all the fuckin' danger of having you guys in my back pocket but none of the safety.

HOLDAWAY

What's the matter, Newendyke? Job too tough for ya? No one lied to you. You always knew we'd hang back until Joe Cabot showed up.

FREDDY

Oh, this is great. You ain't giving me no fuckin' protection whatsoever. But you are giving me an attitude.

HOLDAWAY

Since when does an undercover cop have protection? Freddy, you came into this thing with your eyes wide open, so don't start screamin' blind man now. I understand you're nervous. I wish the warehouse had more visible windows, but it doesn't. We have to make do with the cards we're dealt.

FREDDY

I didn't say I wasn't gonna do it. I'm just remarking on how shitty the situation is!

* Cut from completed film.

HOLDAWAY

I don't mean to be harsh with ya, but I've found tough love works best in these situations. We have to get Joe Cabot in the company of the thieves and in the same vicinity as the loot. We don't care about these other bastards. We're willing to offer them good deals to testify against Cabot.

FREDDY

Isn't this risk unorthodox?

HOLDAWAY

What?

FREDDY

Letting them go ahead with the robbery?

HOLDAWAY

The whole idea behind this operation is to catch Joe Cabot red-handed. We bust these hired hands, we ain't accomplished shit. Letting them go through with the heist is a risk, but Cabot's jobs are very clean. We got people surrounding the perimeter. We got a guy and a gal on the inside posing as a couple shopping for rings. We could replace the employees with cops, but we'd run the risk of tipping 'em off.

FREDDY

That's out. They know the faces of who works what shift.

HOLDAWAY

These guys are professionals. We're professionals. It's a risk, but I think it's a calculated risk.]

EXT. KARINA'S FINE JEWELRY – DAY

We see shots without sound, of the outside of the jewelry store.

Customers coming and going. Store clerks waiting on customers through the windows.

While we look at this we hear, over the soundtrack, Mr White and Freddy talking off screen.

MR WHITE
(*voiceover*)

Let's go over it. Where are you?

FREDDY
(*voiceover*)

I stand outside and guard the door. I don't let anybody come in or
go out.

MR WHITE
(*voiceover*)

Mr Brown.

FREDDY
(*voiceover*)

Mr Brown stays in the car. He's parked across the street till I give
him the signal, then he pulls up in front of the store.

MR WHITE
(*voiceover*)

Mr Blonde and Mr Blue?

FREDDY
(*voiceover*)

Crowd control. They handle customers and employees in the
display area.

INT. MR WHITE'S CAR (PARKED) – DAY

*Mr White and Freddy sit in a car parked across the street from the jewelry
store, staking it out.*

MR WHITE

Myself and Mr Pink?

FREDDY

You two take the manager in the back and make him give you the
diamonds. We're there for those stones, period. Since no display
cases are being fucked with, no alarms should go off. We're out of
there in two minutes, not one second longer. What if the manager
won't give up the diamonds?

MR WHITE

When you're dealing with a store like this, they're insured up the ass. They're not supposed to give you any resistance whatsoever. If you get a customer or an employee who thinks he's Charles Bronson, take the butt of your gun and smash their nose in. Drops 'em right to the floor. Everyone jumps, he falls down, screaming, blood squirts out his nose. Freaks everybody out. Nobody says fuckin' shit after that. You might get some bitch talk shit to ya. But give her a look, like you're gonna smash her in the face next. Watch her shut the fuck up. Now if it's a manager, that's a different story. The managers know better than to fuck around. So if one's givin' you static, he probably thinks he's a real cowboy. So what you gotta do is break that son-of-a-bitch in two. If you wanna know something and he won't tell you, cut off one of his fingers. The little one. Then you tell 'im his thumb's next. After that he'll tell ya if he wears ladies underwear. I'm hungry, let's get a taco.

CUT TO:

EXT. ALLEY – DAY

It's the moment of the robbery. The alley is empty.

In the distance we hear all hell breaking loose. Guns firing, people shouting and screaming, sirens wailing, glass breaking . . .

A car whips around the corner, into the alley.
The doors burst open, Freddy and Mr White hop out.

Freddy opens the driver's side door. A bloody screaming Mr Brown falls out.

MR BROWN
(*screaming*)
My eyes! My eyes! I'm blind, I'm fucking blind!

FREDDY
You're not blind, there's just blood in your eyes.

Mr White loads his two .45 automatics. He runs to the end of the alley just as a police car comes into sight.

Firing both .45s, Mr White massacres everyone in the patrol car.

Freddy, holding the dying Mr Brown, looks on at Mr White's ambush in shock.

Mr Brown lifts his head up, blood in his eyes.

MR BROWN

Mr Orange? You're Mr Orange, aren't you?

By the time Freddy turns his head back to him, Mr Brown is dead.

Mr White runs up to Freddy.

MR WHITE

Is he dead?

Freddy doesn't answer, he can't.

MR WHITE

Did he die or not?

Freddy, scared.

FREDDY

I'm sorry.

MR WHITE

What? Snap out of it!

Mr White grabs Freddy by the coat and yanks him along as he runs.

They exit the alley and flee down a street.

A car with a female driver comes up on the two men.

Mr White jumps in her path, stopping the car. He points his gun at her.

MR WHITE

Hold it! Hold it! Right there.

Freddy comes towards the driver's side of the car.

The Female Driver comes up with a gun from the glove compartment.

MR WHITE

Get out of the fucking car!

She shoots Freddy in the stomach.

On instinct Freddy brings up his gun and shoots her in the face.

CU – FREDDY

as he falls to the ground he realizes what's happened to him and what he's done.

Mr White drags the dead Female Driver out of the car. He shoves Freddy in the backseat and drives away.

INT. GETAWAY CAR (MOVING) – DAY

Freddy, holding his stomach and doubled over in pain, is crying.

We replay the scene between Freddy and Mr White in the getaway car. Except this time, we never leave Freddy.

> MR WHITE
> *(off)*
>
> Just hold on, buddy boy.

> FREDDY
>
> I'm sorry. I can't believe she killed me . . .

CUT FROM FREDDY IN THE BACKSEAT TO:

*[INT. NICE GUY EDDIE'S CAR (MOVING) – DAY

Mr Pink is behind the wheel, Nice Guy Eddie is in the passenger seat going through the satchel with the diamonds. Mr White is in the backseat. The car is speeding back to the garage.

> EDDIE
> *(looking through the case)*
>
> You know, all things considered, this was pretty successful.

> MR WHITE
>
> I don't believe you just said that.

> EDDIE
>
> No, it was messy as hell, but do you realize how much you got away with? There's over two million dollars worth of diamonds here.

> MR PINK
>
> I love this guy.

* Cut from completed film

EDDIE

Hey, what's done is done. We can all sit around and have a big cry about it or we can deal with the situation at hand.

MR WHITE

The situation at hand isn't that fuckin' satchel. You and Joe have a responsibility to your men.

EDDIE

Hey, it's the best I could do.

MR WHITE

The man is fucking dying.

EDDIE

And I'm telling you, Bonnie'll take care of him.

MR WHITE

He needs a doctor, not a fuckin' nurse.

EDDIE

Ask me how many doctors I called. You wanna embarrass yourself, ask me how many doctors I called.

MR WHITE

Obviously not enough.

EDDIE

Fuck you! You gotta little black book, then whip it out. If not, listen how it is. I called three doctors and couldn't get through to shit. Now, time being a factor, I called Bonnie. Sweet broad, helluva broad, and a registered nurse. Told her a bullshit story, upside; she said bring him to her apartment.

MR WHITE

If he dies I'm holding you personally responsible.

EDDIE

Fuck you, buddy boy! Okay, you wanna play that way. I am personally leaving myself vulnerable with this Bonnie situation. I don't think she'll call the cops, but I don't know for sure. But me being too nice-a-fuckin-guy was willin' to risk it. But no fuckin' more.

(*he grabs his portable phone*)

I'm callin' Bonnie back and tellin' her to forget it. You take care of your friend, you know so much about it.

MR PINK

Goddammnit, will you guys grow up!

EDDIE

I don't need to grow up, my friend. I am a grown up. I'm being responsible, I'm taking care of business.

MR WHITE

Cut the shit! I don't think you called anybody except some cooze you once fucked, who happens to wear orthopaedic shoes. And I don't think that's good enough care for a gut-shot man.

EDDIE

Yeah, well I don't give a flying fuck what you think!

MR PINK
(to Mr White)

Look, he's not sayin' this bitch is gonna operate on him. She's gonna give him better attention than we can until we can get a doctor. Nobody's forgotten about doctors. Joe'll get one in a snap. This is something we're doing in the meantime. I think both of you are actin' like a couple of assholes.

EDDIE

Yeah, right. I arrange a nurse, I leave myself wide open, and I'm an asshole.]

INT. WAREHOUSE – DAY

Medium shot on the door. Nice Guy Eddie, Mr White and Mr Pink walk through it. They stop in their tracks.

We see what they see. Mr Blonde, lying on the ground, shot full of holes. The cop slumped over in his chair, a bloody mess, Mr Orange lying at the cop's feet, holding his wound. Eddie, Mr White and Mr Pink walk into the shot.

EDDIE

What the fuck happened here?

Eddie runs over to his friend Mr Blonde/Toothpick Vic.

MR WHITE
(*to Mr Orange*)

What happened?

MR ORANGE
(*very weakly*)

Blonde went crazy. He slashed the cop's face, cut off his ear and was gonna burn him alive.

EDDIE
(*yelling*)

Who cares what he was gonna do to this fuckin' pig?

Eddie whips out his gun and shoots the cop. The cop and the chair tip over. Eddie stands over him and shoots him once more.

EDDIE
(to Mr Orange)

You were saying he went crazy? Something like that? Worse or better?

MR ORANGE

Look, Eddie, he was pullin' a burn. He was gonna kill the cop and me. And when you guys walked through the door, he was gonna blow you to hell and make off with the diamonds.

MR WHITE
(*to Eddie*)

Uhuh, uhuh, what'd I tell ya? That sick piece of shit was a stone cold psycho.

MR ORANGE
(*to Eddie*)

You could've asked the cop, if you didn't just kill him. He talked about what he was going to do when he was slicing him up.

EDDIE

I don't buy it. It doesn't make sense.

MR WHITE

It makes perfect fuckin' sense to me. Eddie, you didn't see how he acted during the job, we did.

Mr Pink walks over to the cop's body.

MR PINK

He's right about the ear, it's hacked off.

EDDIE
(*to Mr Orange*)

Let me say this out loud, just to get it straight in my mind.
According to you, Mr Blonde was gonna kill you. Then when we
came back, kill us, grab the diamonds, and scram. That's your
story? I'm correct about that, right?

MR ORANGE

Eddie, you can believe me or not believe me, but it's the truth. I
swear on my mother's eternal soul that's what happened.

The camera moves into a closeup of Nice Guy Eddie.

There's a long pause while he rolls over what Mr Orange has said. Finally:

*[EDDIE

You're a fuckin' liar. Now why don't you drop the fuckin' fairy tale
and tell me what really happened?

MR WHITE
(*off*)

He told you what really happened. You just can't deal with it.

MR ORANGE
(*off*)

Okay, you're right, I'm lying. Even though I'm fuckin' dyin' I'm
not above pullin' a fast one. Get rid of Blonde, we share his split –
no, scratch that, I shot him 'cause I didn't like his hair style. I didn't
like his shoes either. If it had just been his hair, I'd've maybe, maybe I
said, let him live. But hair and footwear together, he's a goner.]

EDDIE

The man you killed was just released from prison. He got caught at
a company warehouse full of hot items. He could've walked away.
All he had to do was say my dad's name. But instead he shut his
mouth and did his time. He did four years for us, and he did 'em
like a man. And we were very grateful. So, Mr Orange, you're
tellin' me this very good friend of mine, who did four years for my
father, who in four years never made a deal, no matter what they

* Cut from completed film.

103

dangled in front of him, you're telling me that now, that now this man is free, and we're making good on our commitment to him, he's just gonna decide, right out of the fuckin' blue, to rip us off?

Silence.

Mr Orange, why don't you tell me what really happened?

VOICE

Why? It'll just be more bullshit.

Eddie steps out of his closeup and we see Joe Cabot standing in the warehouse doorway. He walks into the room.

JOE
(pointing to Mr Orange)

This man set us up.

Camera does a 360 around the men.

EDDIE

Daddy, I'm sorry, I don't know what's happening.

JOE

That's okay, Eddie, I do.

MR WHITE

What the fuck are you talking about?

JOE
(pointing at Mr Orange)

That piece of shit. Workin' with the cops.

MR WHITE, MR PINK, EDDIE

What?

JOE

I said this lump of shit is workin' with the LAPD.

MR ORANGE'S POV

Looking up from the floor at everybody.

Joe looks down at Mr Orange.

JOE

Aren't you?

MR ORANGE
(*off*)
I don't have the slightest fuckin' idea what you're talkin about.

MR WHITE
(*very calmly to Joe*)
Joe, I don't know what you think you know, but you're wrong.

JOE
Like hell I am.

MR WHITE
(*very calmly*)
Joe, trust me on this, you've made a mistake. He's a good kid. I understand you're hot, you're super-fuckin' pissed. We're all real emotional. But you're barking up the wrong tree. I know this man, and he wouldn't do that.

JOE
You don't know jack shit. I do. This rotten bastard tipped off the cops and got Mr Brown and Mr Blue killed.

MR PINK
Mr Blue's dead?

JOE

Dead as Dillinger.

EDDIE

The motherfucker killed Vic.

MR WHITE

How do you know all this?

JOE

He was the only one I wasn't a hundred per cent on. I should have my fucking head examined for goin' forward when I wasn't a hundred per cent. But he seemed like a good kid, and I was impatient and greedy and all the things that fuck you up.

MR WHITE
(*screaming*)

That's your proof?

JOE

You don't need proof when you got instinct. I ignored it before, but not no more.

He whips out a revolver and aims it at Mr Orange.

Mr White brings his .45 up at Joe.
Eddie and Mr Pink are shook awake by the flash of firearms.

Eddie raises his gun, pointing it at Mr White.

EDDIE

Have you lost your fucking mind? Put your gun down!

Mr Pink fades into the background, wanting no part of this.

MR WHITE

Joe, you're making a terrible mistake I can't let you make.

EDDIE

Stop pointing your fuckin' gun at Daddy!

We get many different angles of the Mexican standoff.

MEDIUMS ON EVERYBODY

Mr Orange holding his belly, looking from left to right.

Joe pointing down on Mr Orange. Not taking his eyes off him.

Mr White pointing at Joe, looking like he's ready to start firing any minute.

Eddie scared shitless for his father, gun locked on Mr White.

Mr Pink walking backwards, away from the action.

Nobody says anything.

FOUR SHOT
of guys ready for violence. Mr Pink in the background.

> MR PINK
> C'mon, guys, nobody wants this. We're supposed to be fuckin'
> professionals!

Joe raises his head to Mr White.

> JOE
> Larry, I'm gonna kill him.

> MR WHITE
> Joe, if you kill that man, you die next. Repeat, if you kill that man,
> you die next!

> EDDIE
> Larry, we have been friends and you respect my dad and I respect
> you, but I will put fucking bullets right through your heart. You
> put that fucking gun down.

> MR WHITE
> Goddamn you, Joe, don't make me do this.

> EDDIE
> Larry, stop pointing that fucking gun at my dad!

Joe fires three times, hitting Mr Orange with every one.

*Mr White shoots Joe twice in the face. Joe brings his hands up to his face,
screaming, and falls to the ground.*

Eddie fires at Mr White, hitting him three times in the chest.

Mr White brings his gun around to Eddie and shoots him.

The two men fall to their knees, firing at each other.

Eddie collapses, dead.

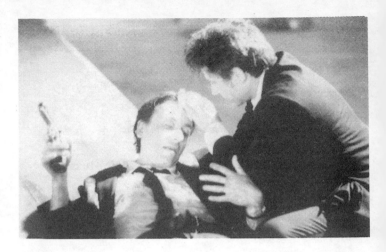

Joe's dead.

Mr Orange lies perfectly still, except for his chest heaving. The only sound we hear is his loud breathing.

Mr White is shot full of holes, but still on his knees, not moving.

Mr Pink is standing motionless. Finally he grabs the satchel of diamonds and runs out the door.

*[We hear outside a car start. Then the sound of a bullhorn yells out:

POLICE FORCE
(*off*)
Freeze! Get out of the car and lie face down on the ground!

MR PINK
(*off*)
Don't shoot!]

We now hear sirens, the sounds of more cars driving up, men running to the warehouse.

While all this noise is going on, Mr White tries to stand but falls down. He somehow makes it to where Mr Orange lies.

* Cut from completed film.

He lifts Mr Orange's head, cradling it in his lap and stroking his brow.

MR WHITE
(*with much effort*)
Sorry, kid. Looks like we're gonna do a little time.

Mr Orange looks up at him and, with even more of an effort:

MR ORANGE
I'm a cop.

Mr White doesn't say anything, he keeps stroking Orange's brow.

I'm sorry, I'm so sorry.

Mr White lifts his .45 and places the barrel between Mr Orange's eyes. The camera moves into an extreme closeup of Mr White.

The sounds of outside storm inside. We don't see anything, but we hear a bunch of shotguns cocking.

POLICE FORCE
(*off*)
Freeze, motherfucker! Drop your fucking gun! Drop the gun! Don't do it!

Mr White looks up at them, smiles, pulls the trigger.

BANG

We hear a burst of shotgun fire.

Mr White is blown out of frame, leaving it empty.

Live America Inc.
A Dog Eat Dog Production
A Film by Quentin Tarantino
RESERVOIR DOGS

HARVEY KEITEL	Mr White [Larry]
TIM ROTH	Mr Orange [Freddy]
MICHAEL MADSEN	Mr Blonde [Vic]
CHRIS PENN	Nice Guy Eddie
STEVE BUSCEMI	Mr Pink
LAWRENCE TIERNEY	Joe Cabot
RANDY BROOKS	Holdaway
KIRK BALTZ	Marvin Nash
EDDIE BUNKER	Mr Blue
QUENTIN TARANTINO	Mr Brown
RICH TURNER	Sheriffs
DAVID STEEN	
TONY COSMO	
STEVE POLIY	
MICHAEL SOTTILE	Teddy
ROBERT RUTH	Shot Cop
LAWRENCE BENDER	Young Cop
LINDA KAYE	Shocked Woman
SUZANNE CELESTE	Shot Woman
STEVEN WRIGHT	K-Billy DJ
LAURIE LATHAM	Radio Play Background Voices
MARIA STROVA	
BURR STEERS	
CRAIG HAMANN	
LAWRENCE BENDER	

Executive Producers	RICHARD N. GLADSTEIN
	RONNA B. WALLACE
	MONTE HELLMAN
Producer	LAWRENCE BENDER
Co-producer	HARVEY KEITEL
Production Co-ordinator	ENID L. KANTOR
Production Manager	PAUL HELLERMAN

Location Manager	BILLY A. FOX
Casting	RONNIE YESKEL
	Associate: PEGGY KENNEDY
	Extras: STAR CASTING
	MARY SANTIAGO
Assistant Directors	JAMIE BEARDSLEY
	FRANCIS R. MAHONY III
	KELLY KIERNAN
	ANDY SPILKOMAN
	STEVEN K. THOMAS
Screenplay	QUENTIN TARANTINO
Background Radio Dialogue	QUENTIN TARANTINO
	ROGER AVERY
Director of Photography	ANDRZEJ SEKULA (In colour)
2nd Unit Photography	ALAN SHERROD
Steadicam Operator	MARK MOORE
Editor	SALLY MENKS
Production Designer	DAVID WASCO
Set Decorator	SANDY REYNOLDS-WASCO
Special Effects Co-ordinator	LARRY FIORITTO
Key Special Effects	PAT DOMENICO
Special Effects	STEVE DELOLLIS
	RICK YALE
Music Supervisors	KARYN RACHTMAN
	MCA: KATHY NELSON
Music/Songs	'Little Green Bag' by Jan Gerbrand Visser, Benjamino Bouwens, performed by George Baker Selection; 'Stuck in the Middle with You' by Gerry Rafferty, Joe Egan, performed by Stealer's Wheel; 'I Gotcha' by and performed by Joe Tex; 'Fool for Love' by and performed by Sandy Rogers; 'Hooked on a Feeling' by Mark James, performed by Blue Suede; 'Coconut' by and performed by Harry Nilsson;

'Harvest Moon' by Jay Joyce, performed by Bedlam; 'Magic Carpet Ride' by Rushton Moreve, John Kay, performed by Bedlam; 'Wes Turned Country' by Nikki Bernard; 'Country's Cool' by Peter Morris; 'It's Country' by Henrik Nielson

Costume Design	BETSY HEIMANN
Costume Supervisor	MARY CLAIRE HANNAN
Set Costumer	JACQUELINE ARONSON
Make-up Artist	MICHELLE BUHLER
Special Make-up Effects	KNB EFX GROUP
Titles/Opticals	TITLE HOUSE, INC.
Supervising Sound Editors	STEPHEN H. FLICK
	GEOFFREY G. RUBAY
Sound Editors	CURT SCHULKEY
	CHUCK SMITH
	DAVE STONE
Sound Recordists	KEN SEGAL
	DAVE MORENO
	MATTHEW C. BELVILLE
	MARK COFFEY
	Foley: CECILIA PERNA
	Dolby Stereo Consultant:
	STEVE F. B. SMITH
Sound Re-recordist	RON BARTLETT
Foley	MARY LOUISE RODGERS
	MICHAEL A. SALVETTA
Production Assistants	WENDY BAKER
	MOSES ROBINSON
	SCOTT SAMPLER
	ELIZABETH TREADWELL
	Post-production:
	JENNIFER PYKEN
Stunt Co-ordinator	KEN LESCO

Stunts	MARIAN GREEN
	MARCIA HOLLEY
	KEN LESCO
	PAT McGROARTY
Animal Handler	NICHOLAS TOTH

113